EXPERIMENT IN LIBERTY

Experiment in Liberty:
The Ideal of Freedom in the Experience of the Disciples of Christ

by Ronald E. Osborn

The Forrest F. Reed Lectures for 1976

The Bethany Press
St. Louis, Missouri

By the Author

In Christ's Place: Christian Ministry in Today's World, 1967
Disciples and the Church Universal, with Robert O. Fife and
   David Edwin Harrell, Jr., 1967
A Church for These Times, 1965
*Restructure . . . Toward the Christian Church: Intention, Es-
   sence, Constitution,* 1964
The Reformation of Tradition, edited 1963
   Vol. I, *The Renewal of the Church: The Panel Reports,* W. B.
      Blakemore, General Editor
The Spirit of American Christianity, 1958
*Ely Vaughn Zollars, Teacher of Preachers, Builder of Colleges:
   A Biography,* 1947

Library of Congress Cataloging in Publication Data

Osborn, Ronald E
   Experiment in liberty.

   (The Forrest F. Reed lectures for 1976)
   Includes bibliographical references and index.
   1.   Christian Church (Disciples of Christ)—United
States—History—Addresses, essays, lectures.
2.   Freedom (Theology)—Addresses, essays, lectures.
I.   Title.   II.   Series: The Reed lectures for 1976.
BX7316.O8   287'.673   77-21273
ISBN 0-8272-0804-9

Printed in the United States of America
Distributed in Canada by The G. R. Welch Company, Ltd.,
Toronto, Ontario, Canada.

Dedicated in Gratitude
for the Friendship of three Kindred Spirits

J. Edward Moseley
Henry K. Shaw
Claude E. Spencer

who led in the Founding of
The Disciples of Christ Historical Society

CONTENTS

1. SPIRIT OF A FREE PEOPLE

The Democratic Ethos of Disciples of Christ

2. LIBERATING THE HUMAN SPIRIT

Some Personal Dimensions of Freedom

3. FREEDOM FOR A UNITED CHURCH

The Integrity of the People of God

FOREWORD

When we invited Ronald E. Osborn to give the Forrest F. Reed Lectures for 1976, we were rather certain what he would do. But we really did not anticipate how well he would do it. The publication of *Experiment in Liberty* now makes it possible for everyone to share the anticipation of the Reed Lectures committee and to join with us in celebration of a job well done.

Writing an introduction to Carter E. Boren's *Religion on the Texas Frontier* (Naylor), the late dean of Disciple historians, W. E. Garrison said that "sound historical generalizations must be based upon an accumulation of many particular facts." In that same introduction Garrison spoke of his own writing some years earlier about the way to understand pioneers on the frontier. He asked the questions: "What ideas had these pioneers brought with them; what concepts and presuppositions had they inherited; how were they related to the currents of religious life and thought which had flowed to them out of the past? What influences played upon them and their successors, and with what result, as the frontier conditions under which the movement originated were transformed by the cultural and economic changes that their century brought?"

Ronald Osborn has certainly accumulated "many particular facts." I no longer recall when I began going around with him to various historical, denominational, and ecumenical activities but it was about the time that he came out of the University of Oregon with a doctorate in medieval history. He is my junior by some years but it was easy to observe that he was in the mold of anecdotal historians (I refer to such as Garrison and Bainton of Yale). When you get enough of these little incidents together you have the stuff of historical generalizations. The tendency of some who write history in a hurry is to state one general principal for every two incidents observed, when they should have waited for a thousand.

In this regard, *Experiment in Liberty* is full of stories and characterizations; it is easy to read. We don't need to be much beyond voting age to hear stories which we recognize. And for those of us who have walked longer paths toward the sunset most of the incidents are familiar. That is why they are fun to read! But the author never paints himself into a corner where he must state a conclusion without sufficient grounds for doing so.

Not everyone could get Sally Rand, John Wooden, Carry Nation, the "Veep," General Bradley and Charles Kirbo into the same story. What the writer does is to contribute enough stories and information to enable the reader to follow him in his conclusion that Disciples are ordinary folks. They have all partaken of the frontier spirit to greater or lesser degrees, not only as citizens of the new world but also as Disciples. The influence runs in both directions, from society to the church and from the religious convictions to participation in society.

As one reads along and finds more and more familiar material he might be inclined to wonder what the fuss is all about. Why reiterate a tale that has been told ofttimes, not only by the author but by others in part or in full? Then, when he states a particular interest for this series of lectures during America's Bicentennial year, the distinctiveness of his approach becomes apparent.

Osborn is writing about liberty! Let freedom ring! But he isn't a flag-waver, actually. He makes a modest approach to an element in Disciple thought and life which he believes to have been overlooked, or insufficiently stressed—the emphasis on liberty.

Anyone familiar with early Disciple history knows about the twin emphases—unity and restoration. Some have stressed one or the other and in their thinking, others have become "biased." The "others," in turn, have been sure that they took a properly mixed dose of both of the concerns of the fathers. Osborn does little with these two ideas except to show that they have been dominant themes in the development of all three divisions of Discipledom which now exist. He is interested in developing the story of a third major aspect of thought which he believes to have been present from the earliest days—freedom.

This author's interest in liberty is all-encompassing. Furthermore, he sees this religious movement as one in which the persons involved expressed the spirit of a free people in all aspects of life, personal and social. It isn't as if a religious group sought to influence politics or the social ethics of the time. As he sees it, "Liberating the Human Spirit," to use the title of the second lecture, consists in championing human freedom in every aspect of life.

Freedom enables individuals to respond to the Gospel; Disciples have always objected to creeds as tests of fellowship, but not as statements of what the formulators believed. Freedom has made possible the educational system of the church, in the congregation and on the campus. The educational system, in turn, has created ever new generations who exercise freedom with responsibility, in the political area, in the church structures, and in the community.

A final word should be said about Osborn's end purpose in expounding this belief that Disciples are a people who espouse liberty. The title of the third lecture tells where he has been heading—"Freedom for a United Church." In this chapter he reiterates Disciple thought on unity, connecting current endeavors with the position of the fathers. He sees Disciple anti-creedalism, anti-clericalism and anti-ecclesiasticism, not as hindrances to unity but rather as an expression of that sort of freedom that must be present in all parties seeking to reunite the church.

In short, this seminary professor who has always been an activist in the best sense of the word, one who served as the first Moderator of the restructured Christian Church (Disciples of Christ), is ready for a united church. And he thinks he has something to offer in the discussions from his Disciple heritage and current practice.

We agree with him and it has been a pleasure to serve as chairman of the Reed Lecture Committee, along with Mrs. Mary Smith and Claude Walker, in extending the invitation to Dr. Osborn to produce a set of lectures appropriate for a bicentennial.

He understands "this particular slice" of church life very well and he has not been forced to overdraw the true historical picture of our Disciple forefathers in order to have them a part of the bicentennial story of freedom. The data tell the story and Dr. Osborn is acquainted with both. He has met the committee's challenge and the lectures are now before you in book form. They will be easy to read and to enjoy; their implications will be as difficult to carry out as ever.

Howard E. Short
Interim President
Division of Higher Education,
Christian Church (Disciples of Christ)

PREFACE

Two hundred years ago the people of the United States laid claim to their freedom. In asserting that right they launched a revolution with worldwide repercussions. To validate their title to political liberty, they used language both absolute and universal, both realistically secular and profoundly religious. Because they were human, vision outran performance in extending liberty and justice to all. Yet gradually, if sometimes grudgingly, their children have broadened the range of freedom, convinced by the logic and the rhetoric of the founders' dream. For two centuries the love of liberty, however variously they have conceived it, has stirred the hearts of Americans. It touches, even if it fails to control, every aspect of their life and thought.

Devotion to freedom has quickened the spirit and shaped the forms of religion no less than it has enlivened other aspects of the culture. Edward Scribner Ames observed that "in America, for the first time, Christianity has come under the influence of a democratic society." As a result, Americans have infused the life of church and synagogue with the democratic ethos. Sensitized by their environment, they have drawn from the biblical tradition implications for liberty which previous generations, living under various forms of autocracy, had failed to see. Preoccupation with freedom became a characteristic aspect of religion in early America, profoundly affecting the way in which the various ecclesiastical bodies developed. Some, like the Baptists and the radical sectarians, came to this country already committed to liberty in church and state. Others— Roman Catholics, Anglicans, Lutherans, Presbyterians—welcomed the guarantee of civil liberties in the United States, then struggled to reshape theology and ecclesiastical government to accord with the spirit of a free people. Other religious bodies were born in this free land. One of these, intensely committed to liberty throughout its history, is that movement whose members call themselves Disciples of Christ.[1]

An invitation from the Disciples of Christ Historical Society to deliver the Forrest F. Reed Lectures in the nation's Bicentennial year intensified my thoughts about the importance of freedom in the history of this movement, and I determined to explore the involvement of this representative body of American Christians with the great ideal. The devotion of Disciples to freedom is not unique among religious groups in this land, nor do I argue that they have made a larger contribution than others in understanding it. But constant awareness of their love for liberty is essential to understanding *them*. It rang as a stirring note through their original documents, it animated their efforts in the days of their dramatic growth in the American heartland, and it continues to dominate their temperament.

Oddly enough, no historian of the Disciples has traced the ideal of freedom through the history of the movement. (This in spite of the fact that in the days when they commonly spoke of "First Principles" they included liberty among them.)[2] Even more striking is the general tendency of historians, aside from an occasional mention of freedom and the assumption that everyone knows the Disciples' commitment to it, to omit it from the basic formula of interpretation. It has become conventional to present the movement as concerned with two great emphases, *unity* and *restoration*.[3]

In my view, the effort to understand Disciples in terms of these two principles alone (or of either one of them) oversimplifies the situation. The commitment of heart and mind was not just to unity, not just to restoration of the apostolic order, not just to some dynamic combination of these two. From the beginning that commitment was given to freedom, unity, and restoration, held together in a varying and sometimes unstable equilibrium. Indeed, one could advance the thesis that freedom has now become the dominant force within the triad. Within the Christian Church (Disciples of Christ), as within the undenominational fellowship of Christian Churches and Churches of Christ, the most compelling argument against any proposal is neither that it is divisive nor that it is unscriptural, but that it threatens the freedom of the congregation or infringes on the rights of the members. My selection of the motif of liberty is not a Bicentennial gimmick; rather it seizes an appropriate occasion for the exposition of a major theme running through the life of the movement.[4]

My purpose here, then, is to examine the history of Disciples of Christ in the United States under the rubric of freedom. The approach is thematic, as dictated by the form of a lectureship. Though I include here some material not presented in oral delivery, this brief volume only announces a lode to be worked; it does not exhaust the vein. Perhaps the glint of gold may lure some future scholars to more systematic investigation.

The title *Experiment in Liberty* intends to suggest that process of testing which the historian sees constantly going on in the experience of any group. While insistence on freedom has

13

been a dominant strain in the Disciples' self-consciousness, the ways in which they undertook to guarantee it or bring it to expression have changed dramatically. In religion as elsewhere, experience is an effective teacher, and Disciples have learned from it.

The term Disciples in these pages refers to the founders of the movement and, in a general way, to all their successors in three now disparate groups: the Churches of Christ, the undenominational fellowship of Christian Churches and Churches of Christ, and the Christian Church (Disciples of Christ.) In dealing with more recent developments, most of my attention centers on the third of these groups, primarily because of my more intimate acquaintance and deeper involvement. Yet I hold to the conviction that all three seek to continue the early commitment to liberty, however variously they have undertaken to secure it in the life of the church. There is no single line of thought among Disciples on any issue, as the most eminent social historian of the movement has observed. While I have not searched out all the variations, nor is there space to present them here, I have set forth what I take to be the preponderant and characteristic view.[5]

The format of a lectureship has determined the nature of this presentation—somewhat informal and, it is to be hoped, popular, though dealing with issues of substance. To maintain some objective distance as a historian, I consistently refer to Disciples as "they" rather than as "we." This is an exercise in exposition and analysis rather than propaganda, yet it comes from a church historian who is a committed participant, not just a detached observer.

My roots in this tradition grow deep. My great-great-grandparents responded to the preaching of one of Walter Scott's collaborators in the Mahoning Baptist Association. William and Sophia Lanterman were members of the church at Austintown, Ohio when the association voted to dissolve and the Reformers became Disciples. They are buried in the churchyard of that historic rural congregation, in which three generations after them also held membership. On the other side of the family my people were active Disciples, my Grandmother Osborn being one of the leading spirits in the local auxiliary of the Christian Woman's Board of Missions. I grew up in a minister's home, catching the spirit of congregations in the American Southwest and in Great Britain. When our family moved to Virginia in my adolescent years, a number of congregations in the Old Dominion were celebrating their centennials. My father chaired the editorial committee which produced the history of the churches in Richmond, and at an impressionable age I listened to B. A. Abbott, Peter Ainslie, and A. W. Fortune interpret this movement.[6] While I was still a boy my father put me to the reading of biographies, including the lives of eminent Disciples. At Phillips University I learned much of the tradition, formally and informally, from Frank Hamilton Marshall and Stephen J. England. There in Oklahoma, settled then for less than fifty years, I caught the ethos of the movement from the prairie saints among whom I began to preach.

After a pastorate in Arkansas, my wife and I spent three years with the Christian Board of Publication in close association with Glenn McRae, Raphael H. Miller, and Lin D. Cartwright and in constant contact with other leaders of the brotherhood. In the Bethany Book Store I was able to pick up scores of volumes, many of them long out of print, bearing on the witness of this movement. In 1946 I began to teach church history, first in college, then in seminary, and in most of those years I have offered work on the history of Disciples. The churches in Oregon celebrated their centennial while we lived there. In Indiana we shared the life of scores of congregations, the friendship of the leaders of the brotherhood across more than two decades, and a heavy involvement in the reexamination of the heritage and in the restructure which led in 1968 to the reconstituting of the Christian Church (Disciples of Christ). Now we are entering into the tradition of Disciples in California. All of this experience, with extended reflection on it from the perspective of one deeply involved in ecumenical dialogue, has deepened my conviction of the importance of freedom as a major component of the Disciple ethos.

I am grateful to the lectureship committee and to the Trustees of the Disciples of Christ Historical Society for the invitation to present the Forrest F. Reed Lectures in 1976, a year of particular symbolism. (As the principal of a junior high school recently told his pupils, a nation doesn't get to observe its Bicentennial very often!) Roland K. Huff, President of the Society, extended every courtesy as host and worked tirelessly to bring the lectures to publication. David I. McWhirter, Director of the Library and Archives, cheerfully and efficiently tracked down rare books.

In connection with this first lectureship since the death of the donor and because of the high personal regard in which I held him, I enter a note of appreciation for that remarkable Christian layman, Forrest Reed. In 1951 the Disciples of Christ Historical Society was a shoestring operation with a great vision, operating in space donated by Culver-Stockton College on time contributed by its sole staff member, Claude E. Spencer, the college librarian. In that year a group of daring spirits in Nashville offered to put the Society on its financial feet by raising a fund to move it to that city, maintain its operation for an initial period, and house its collection for a time in the Joint University Libraries. Forrest Reed was a moving spirit and the Maecenas of that venture. He contributed generously and solicited effectively in order to raise the initial Nashville grant of $55,000. As a member of the Board and the Executive Committee of the Society, he gave unreservedly of his energy and business acumen from the time of the move, through the erection of the Phillips Memorial building, and across the ensuing years until his death. In 1964 he initiated the lectureship which bears his name, in order to encourage new investigation by historians of the Disciples and their presentation to Nashville audiences. It is fitting that the first lecture of the 1976 series was given at Woodmont Christian Church, where Mr. and Mrs. Reed worshiped and served. He devoted much effort to the Society's program of publication, in which his experience as a publisher and bookman proved an invaluable asset. Always a gracious host and faithful friend, he gave us cause for gratitude beyond expression. As president of the Society at the time of the move to Nashville, I worked closely with him, and I honor the memory of Forrest Reed.[7]

Appreciation is due to the School of Theology at Claremont for the sabbatical leave during which these lectures were prepared and delivered. I am particularly grateful to Dean Donald D. Reisinger of the Disciples Seminary Foundation for his encouragement, to Mildred Whitworth and Mary Anne Parrott of the Foundation staff for their work in typing the final copy of this material, under great pressure of time, and to Harold E. Fey for judicious comments on the manuscript. I remember gladly those students in Northwest Christian College, Christian Theological Seminary, and the School of Theology at Claremont who have explored with me the history of Disciples of Christ. Out of reflection with them have come many of the insights here presented. As in all my work, my wife Naomi has given constant encouragement, support, and insight. A free spirit long before women's liberation, she combines more than any one I know the strength of personal independence with intense loyalty.

The biblical verse at the head of each lecture comes from the new translation published by Alexander Campbell in 1826 and popularly known by its binder's title as *The Living Oracles*. This was one of the earliest modern-speech translations of the

16

New Testament. Scripture used elsewhere comes from the Revised Standard Version, unless otherwise indicated.[8]

This book is dedicated to three friends who were moving spirits in the founding and maturing of the Disciples of Christ Historical Society and each of whom contributed much to my own development.

J. Edward Moseley (1910-1973) was assistant editor of *The Christian-Evangelist* in the summer of 1939 when as a seminarian I took advantage of a lay-over between trains in St. Louis to visit the offices of the Christian Board of Publication. He extended generous hospitality, discovered my interest in Disciple history, and talked enthusiastically about it. He began to direct writing assignments my way, solicited my support for the Disciples of Christ Historical Society after its founding in 1941 (he was its first president), and in due time involved me more deeply in its life. Together we made numerous trips to Nashville, worked closely on various committees of the Society, and enjoyed extended conversations on the history and lore of Disciples. He and Louise were faithful friends to Naomi and me and to our daughter Virginia. To the life and literature of the movement he made a distinguished contribution.[9]

Claude E. Spencer dreamed for years of a historical society for the Disciples, collected Discipliana with zeal, and served as curator of DCHS from the time of its founding until his retirement. I visited the Society's humble operation at Culver-Stockton College and shared with him in the excitement of the move to Nashville, the trials in getting the Society on its financial feet, and the elation at the dedication of the Thomas W. Phillips Memorial. In the early days, when the Board was made up of penniless history buffs, the high point of our meetings was not the business session but Spencer's guided tour through the archives to point out new acquisitions and to encourage our professorial gloating. Times beyond counting he responded to my requests for information which could have come from nowhere else. His knowledge of the sources of this history is encyclopedic, his bibliographical contributions are heroic in scale, and the great collection of Discipliana in Nashville stands as a monument to his dedication.[10]

Serving as a member of the Campbell Home Committee in 1951 I began a close association with Henry K. Shaw, whom I had already met and whose wit as author of the classic piece about the Alexander Campbell Cigar had already brought delight to me and my students. Early in my days at Christian Theological Seminary he joined our faculty as librarian, and a fast friendship grew. Hardly a day passed that I did not stop in the library office to converse about common interests. We stood by one another in dark days and in many times of joy. I have learned much from his histories, *Buckeye Disciples* and *Hoosier Disciples*. For nearly twenty years I called upon him to go over every article or lecture I wrote about Disciples; always its focus was sharpened and its accuracy improved by his discerning comment. I regret only that our present situations with a continent between us prevented my offering these lectures to his scrutiny before delivery. One could not ask for a more faithful friend.[11]

These three have made a major contribution to the work of American church historians, especially to those whose studies center on Disciples of Christ. They did far more for me than I can ever repay.

These lectures address a vital theme. David Brinkley recently observed that "only 19 percent of the people on earth live in what we would call freedom, and this small number gets smaller all the time." We do well to give attention to it, not with mere ceremonial tribute, but in renewal of dedication. Norman Cousins commented about the Bicentennial: "The nation has celebrated everything except the Revolution itself." Like the founders of the Republic, Disciples too were rebels. And in both cases the revolt led to new institutions intended to serve the cause of liberty. I trust that this book may contribute to the extension of that good cause.[12]

Claremont, California
November, 1976

1. Spirit of a Free People
The Democratic Ethos of Disciples of Christ

For you . . . have been called into liberty
—Galatians 5:13

A generation after the American Revolution old Sam Adams still stumped about the streets of Boston stubbornly wearing a cocked hat. Among his fellow citizens the tricorn of 1776 had long since given way to newer styles of headgear. Busy Bostonians intent upon their trade smiled not altogether approvingly at the old radical striking his anachronistic pose of defiance against King George.[1]

Frontier Democracy

But if Boston had already become a bastion of commerce and conservatism, the mood of the revolution still quickened the pulses of the folk beyond the mountains. In the new settlements filling up the valleys of the interior rivers and swelling into young towns along the new National Road, an agrarian people still asserted the spirit of independence. A tattered manuscript in the archives of the Indiana Historical Society records thirteen toasts prepared for the celebration of the Glorious Fourth. I select a few:

1   *The day we celebrate . . .*
      . . . Sacred to every lover of Freedom . . . May it never be profaned by an unhallowed thought or action

2   *The Declaration of Independence . . .*
    A Manifesto dictated by the spirit and finger of God . . .

4   *The surviving Revolutionary Fathers here and there lingering amongst us like guardian spirits . . .*

In the election of 1800 these liberty-loving farmers of the frontier awarded the presidency to the author of the Declaration of Independence. Within three years Thomas Jefferson had negotiated the Louisiana Purchase, doubling the area of the United States and enhancing the potential strength of the West. An exciting sense of destiny thrilled in the veins of these people.[3]

The rude schools and colleges of the interior imparted to the rising generation the axioms of the Enlightenment. If the settlers had little sympathy for the radicalism of the French Revolution and little knowledge of newer intellectual currents in the sophisticated centers of Europe, they nevertheless gave themselves to vigorous thought on issues that concerned them. Lewis and Clark went up the Missouri in 1804, across the Great Divide the next spring, and down the Columbia to the Pacific, diligently recording the topography of the Continent and its possibilities for settlement. John James Audubon had already begun his studies of the birds of America. The pioneers understandably prized such practical uses of natural science or a knowledge of surveying above the traditional disciplines of the schools.[4] But whether formally educated or not, they endlessly discussed certain majestic ideas, especially the theory and practice of liberty.

Toward the end of the second generation after the Revolution, Robert Dale Owen (son of the celebrated social reformer who had debated Alexander Campbell) spoke in the Congress of the United States about these pioneers. Their conversation, said he, had depth. It delved below the surface of current events to get at basic principles of constitutional theory.

I have heard in many a backwoods cabin, lighted but by the blazing log heap, arguments on government, views of national policy, judgments of men and things, that, for sound sense and practical wisdom, would not disgrace any legislative body upon earth.[5]

Fifty years after the Revolution—on July 4, 1826—death came to John Adams and Thomas Jefferson on the same day. But a new champion of the people was already waiting in the wings. Two years later the voters of the West teamed up with the workers of the Eastern cities to give the presidency to Andrew

Jackson. "And he snorted 'freedom' and it flashed from his eye."[6] Not from the eye of Old Hickory alone, however. In the new era of Jacksonian Democracy the love of liberty was the light that gleamed from the eyes of a people.

Disciples on the Frontier

From such a people Barton Stone came. Born on the seaboard in 1772, he grew up on the frontier and came to Kentucky as a Presbyterian pastor at the age of 24. Among such a people Thomas Campbell began to minister in western Pennsylvania in 1807. The state claimed well over 120,000 persons of Scottish blood, and five out of every six of these, like Campbell himself, were Scotch-Irish. Relishing taxes levied by the young Congress no better than those imposed by the old Parliament, the inhabitants of four western counties had unleashed the Whiskey Rebellion in 1794. (One of these was Washington County, destined to be the base of Thomas Campbell's labors.)[7] Among such people young Alexander Campbell arrived in 1809 and Walter Scott in 1818. It was the liberty-loving people of the Western waters who rallied to the evangelical banners raised by Stone and the Campbells and Scott. These folk established the positions and attitudes of the Disciples of Christ.

W. E. Garrison has characterized the enterprise of the Disciples as "An American Religious Movement," and an environmental determinist could readily interpret their venture as an ecclesiastical and theological parallel to the national political experiment. It would be too simple to say that Jacksonian Democracy and the position of the Disciples were simply two alternative vocabularies, the one political and the other religious, both asserting the same thing. But we do well to remember that the folk who first responded to the "Plea" were daughters and sons of the revolution, both by disposition and by conviction or they were more recent immigrants to the new nation, who espoused its political commitments with no less fervor than those born on American soil. All these ardent devotees of the civil liberty guaranteed by the Constitution of the United States exercised their freedom of choice to enlist in the religious reformation proclaimed by Alexander Campbell and his co-laborers. They believed that both ventures were consistent, that both represented the purpose of God. And they gave their hearts both to the new nation and the restored church with no sense of strain between the two.

Pioneer Disciples as Champions of Freedom

The churchly vision of this freedom-loving people will occupy us later as the theme of our third lecture, but we lift up some aspects of it now simply to underscore the pervasiveness of liberty throughout their whole scheme of values.

Freedom-Loving Christians

The earliest of the American movements of religious revolt to contribute significantly to the rise of the Disciples was that of Methodist James O'Kelly. At the famed Christmas Conference of 1784, the American Wesleyans elected Francis Asbury as superintendent, but he straightway assumed the title of bishop and began to construct the remarkably effective system of the Methodist episcopate in America. And straightway O'Kelly began to resist this new departure in ecclesiastical authority. When the first General Conference met in 1792 he offered a motion to qualify the bishop's powers of assigning preachers to circuits. Under his proposal any minister who considered himself injured by an announced appointment could exercise "liberty to appeal" to the conference as a whole, which might then direct the bishop to arrange a different appointment. When the motion failed, O'Kelly withdrew, along with Rice Haggard and other Southern preachers, to form the Republican Methodist Church. Before long Haggard persuaded them to change the name to Christian Church. O'Kelly's *Apology for Protesting Against the Methodist Episcopal Government* appealed to the "Royal Standard" of Scripture as the charter of ecclesiastical freedom.[8]

Meanwhile on the theological front, the Freewill Baptists emerged in New England to protest the rigid Calvinist doctrine of election. As their name implied, they taught the freedom of a person to believe and accept the gospel. They felt themselves spiritually akin to the newly emerging Christian Churches in their area and ordained a number of ministers for that "connection." When Abner Jones received ordination from three of their ministers in 1802, it was not as a Freewill Baptist but "only as a Christian." Later on in the South and West some of their congregations became "Churches of Christ." In 1808 Jones' colleague Elias Smith launched a religious newspaper, one of the first in America. He named it the *Herald of Gospel Liberty*.[9]

In 1804 when Barton W. Stone and the other revival men in

the Synod of Kentucky issued *The Last Will and Testament of the Springfield Presbytery* they stated a similar vision: "that the oppressed may go free, and taste the sweets of gospel liberty." Meanwhile Rice Haggard had come West and again he persuaded a little band of ecclesiastical freedom-fighters to adopt the name Christian Church. Before long Stone was in touch with the two movements of Eastern Christians, both North and South. Even though few of them accompanied him a generation later in uniting with the Disciples of Christ, he regarded them as kindred minds.[10]

Thomas Campbell's Manifesto

Thomas Campbell came to America in 1807 and two years later penned his *Declaration and Address,* a platform for the unity of the church on the basis of the plain teaching of Scripture. It was an eloquent protest against ecclesiastical pretensions and their divisive effects. In a medley of familiar biblical phrases he sounded the trumpet of freedom:

"Awake, awake; put on thy strength, O Zion, put on thy beautiful garments, O Jerusalem the holy city; . . . . Shake thyself from the dust, O Jerusalem; arise, loose thyself from the bands of thy neck, O captive daughter of Zion."—Resume that precious, that dear bought liberty, wherewith Christ has made his people free; a liberty from subjection to any authority but his own, in matters of religion. Call no man father, no man master upon earth;—for one is your master, even Christ, and all ye are brethren. Stand fast therefore in this precious liberty, and be not entangled again with the yoke of bondage. For the vindication of this precious liberty have we declared ourselves hearty and willing advocates.

To Campbell's Scotch-Irish constituents, the emphasis on the authority of Christ (which may not sound to contemporary secular ears like the language of a liberationist) awakened echoes of heroic tales about their Scottish ancestors. They had contended for the "Crown Rights of Christ in His Church." To them, "setting Christ on his throne" had meant repudiating all pretensions by any earthly power, civil or ecclesiastical, over the soul of the Christian. Divine sovereignty and Christian liberty were two sides of a coin.[11] In time Disciples took over the old slogan of Rupertus Meldenius to express the essence of Campbell's position:

> *In essentials unity,*
> *in opinions liberty,*
> *in all things charity.*

To Disciples generally, their situation in the young nation provided a heaven-sent opportunity for starting anew—in religion, in government, and in the pursuit of happiness. They saw themselves as godly advocates of freedom on every front. Thomas Campbell spoke glowingly of "a thorough reformation, in all things civil and religious." This phrase stands in a fervent passage in the *Declaration and Address* which clearly affirms the consistency of freedom in the church with freedom in the state. He addresses his fellow ministers:

The favorable opportunity which Divine Providence has put into your hands, in this happy country, for the accomplishment of so great a good, is a consideration of no small encouragement. A country happily exempted from the baneful influence of a civil establishment of any peculiar form of christianity—from under the direct influence of the anti-christian hierarchy—and at the same time, from any formal connection with the devoted nations, that have given their strength and power unto the beast; in which, of course, no adequate reformation can be accomplished, until the word of God is fulfilled, and the vials of his wrath poured out upon them. . . . Can the Lord expect, or require, any thing less, from a people in such unhampered circumstances— from a people so liberally furnished with all means and mercies, than a thorough reformation, in all things civil and religious, according to his word?[12]

The virulent strain of anti-Catholicism which erupts in this ecumenical classic continued to run in the blood of Disciples until the time of the Second Vatican Council. It broke out repeatedly in the utterances of Alexander Campbell: "To be free, nations must be Protestant." One such remark provoked the challenge for the debate with Bishop Purcell of Cincinnati. The intense feeling of both father and son shows the effect of their experience as Protestants in Northern Ireland. However ungracious their language about Rome may sound to us now, we can readily see the reason for its intensity: in their minds the Roman Catholic Church both perverted the gospel and subverted political freedom. "Protestantism and Liberty are like the Siamese twins—united in life and united in death."[13]

Alexander Campbell as Freedom-Advocate

Not long after his own arrival in America young Alexander Campbell began to demonstrate some implications of the principles set forth by his father. He received ordination to the ministry from one independent congregation. Attracted for a time to the Baptists by their fidelity to Scripture and their love

24

of liberty, he emerged after two decades as the leader of a distinct movement on which he more than any other person placed the stamp of his thought. His system incorporated emphases we have already heard: the freedom of the hearer to believe and obey the gospel, the liberty of Christians to hold diverse opinions on matters not revealed, the emancipation of the church from all oppressive structures of human authority whether theological or ecclesiastical. Repeatedly in presenting his position on church order he resorted to analogies with the American political system. He considered the reformation which he led and the new venture of the United States to be parallel and compatible experiments in liberty:

It is not possible, or, in other words, it is not in human nature, to love liberty, freedom of thought, of speech and of action, in the state, and to hate it in the church; or to love it in the church and to hate it in the state.[14]

The commitment of the United States to freedom inspired Campbell to frequent eloquence. He loved his adopted nation and its institutions. "We are the stern, uncompromising advocates of human rights." Like Thomas Jefferson, he faithfully read John Locke, and from the Letters on Toleration drew his theory of civil and religious liberty. He chose to launch his publication *The Christian Baptist* on the Fourth of July, 1823, and he regularly scheduled the commencement festivities at Bethany College on Independence Day. A colorful event in the early history of the movement was an all-day love-feast held in an arbor near Pittsburgh on Monday, July 5, 1830. (The Fourth had fallen on the Lord's Day.) Some 120 Disciples "with sundry visitants and many children" observed the occasion with a patriotic oration by Campbell, a dinner, a sermon on the millennium by Walter Scott, and the immersion of five persons "into the ancient faith." Campbell considered it appropriate, while

"the children of this world" celebrated the nation's independence with "noisy mirth . . . because of the political privileges" they enjoyed, that Christians should give "glory to the Governor of the nations of the earth that they are made free citizens, not only of a free Government on earth, but of the kingdom of heaven."[15]

In his pride of citizenship Campbell visited Washington, D.C. and commended the importance of erecting a worthy house of worship for the Disciples in the nation's capital. He entered the political arena himself, winning election to the Virginia Constitutional Convention in 1829. In the debates against James Madison, James Monroe, John Marshall, and other Eastern

25

aristocrats at that convention and in the campaign for free public education he became the eloquent champion of the democratic frontier counties in their struggle against the Establishment. His evident service to the cause of political liberty won hundreds of admirers and added strength to the progress of his religious reformation.[16]

Carey J. Gifford says of Campbell that "His correlation of democratic faith and Christianity goes so far as to nearly make Christianity a spiritual form of democracy and democracy a secular form of Protestantism." And Ernest Lee Tuveson submits that for Campbell " 'Americanizing' the world, in the right sense, is almost identical with millennializing it." If one accepts some recent theorizing about the secular meaning of religious language, one must admit some validity in such judgments. For Campbell could exult, "We are Republicans and Protestants." The rhetoric in which he expressed devotion to country amounts to an assertion of American civil religion. Yet Campbell did not make the nation ultimate. In his most fervent utterances as a patriot, he took care to distinguish commitment to country from Christian faith: the founder of Christianity "never pronounced a single sentence in commendation" of patriotism.[17]

Indeed, to Campbell, the term *patriot* represented the smallest of three concentric circles of loyalty. The patriot was a lover of one's nation, its institutions, and its people. A broader loyalty made one a *philanthropist,* a lover of all humanity and a devotee of its welfare. But the highest loyalty of all was that of the *Christian,* whose love embraced not only humanity, but God as well. "The patriot, indeed, is absorbed in the philanthropist, and the philanthropist in the Christian." When Campbell preached at the nation's capital in the Hall of Representatives, June 2, 1850, he held forth for an hour and a half on the theme, "Divine Philanthropy."[18]

His love of country ran far deeper than mere secular regard for the nation in which he lived and worked. It was tinged with affection for the land, a God-given source of beauty and wealth. But at its heart it sprang from a belief in the divinely ordered destiny of the United States in furthering the advance both of religious reformation and of freedom. His expressions of this view place his patriotic enthusiasm within a larger regard for the political heritage and Protestant faith derived from Great Britain and Germany. He frequently affirmed the superiority of the Anglo-Saxon peoples and his understanding of their destiny: to extend the sway of freedom. He invoked Luther and Washington in the same breath as heroes of liberty. Indeed, the religious reformation in which he was engaged was not an end in itself. Rather the recovery of the apostolic faith and order would make possible the unity of the church, and *that* the conversion of the world, and *that* in turn the inauguration of the millennium, God's era of universal peace, righteousness, and felicity. His fusion of belief in American destiny with ardent endeavors as a Christian and with social messianism resembles the social outlook of Cotton Mather in the seventeenth century and of Jonathan Edwards in the eighteenth.[19]

Yet Campbell's remarkable social idealism combined with a tough, self-regarding realism not always found in visionaries and prophets. Unabashedly he affirmed the legitimacy, even duty, of self-love on the part of the Christian. In his case, intense religious commitment coexisted comfortably with the building up of a sizeable fortune and the expression of a powerful ambition. He admitted no inconsistency. A Christian philanthropist was a man who loved his neighbor but who also, without apology, loved himself. Nor did Campbell sentimentalize his philanthropy. He admitted that he loved a white man more than a black man, and he saw no impropriety in the admission, for he regarded the white man as superior.[20]

The Great Contradiction

Campbell refused to take an absolute stand as a Christian in opposition to slavery. Accepting the authority of Scripture in all things, he found it impossible to condemn the institution on religious grounds. One's views about it were simply a matter of political and economic opinion; consequently, he taught the impropriety of preaching on the subject. In his personal judgment he regarded slavery as a social evil. He believed that the nation should undertake its gradual elimination. But he was not an abolitionist; rather he held views quite similar to those of Henry Clay and Abraham Lincoln.[21]

Along with Campbell, numbers of Disciples concluded that the answer to the problem was to secure the freedom of as many slaves as possible and send them back to the continent of their ancestors. Elder Ben Major, founder of Walnut Grove Academy (now Eureka College), was a leader in the so-called colonization movement. Mrs. Emily H. Tubman of Augusta, Georgia, pioneer philanthropist among the Disciples, manumitted 69 of her slaves in 1834 and contributed a fund to pay their passage to Africa. A grandson of two of these slaves, W. V. S. Tubman, became the eighteenth president of Liberia in 1941. Other Disciples took an absolute moral stand against slavery, establishing a new Christian Missionary Society on abolitionist principles and new colleges in Indiana and Illinois rather than send their young people to attend Bethany College in a slave state.[22]

Most Disciples, however, simply refused to regard slavery as a religious issue, on the grounds that it was permitted in the New Testament. Thus despite Campbell's evident love for freedom, his eloquent espousal of the institutions of liberty, and his belief in the imminence of the ideal social order (the millennium), he did not sound the trumpet against the most blatant denial of human freedom on the American scene. Disciples generally followed his line in excluding the matter from the area of legitimate churchly concern. We may note several results.

(1) By their stance, Disciples abdicated churchly leadership on the most pressing moral issue of the century.

(2) Disciples thus saved the "brotherhood" from a division over slavery. Their elation at the presumed vindication of their plea for Christian unity blinded them for another century to the sectional character of the schism which began to divide them shortly after the Civil War.

(3) Disciples failed to examine theologically the simple biblicism of Thomas Campbell's slogan, "Where the Scriptures speak...." The appeal to the Bible offered such plausible refuge from the controversy over slavery that they felt no need to develop any more sophisticated procedure. In the subsequent era of controversy they tended either to retain the legalistic approach or to shrug off the authority of the Bible altogether in the questions at issue—even if they long repressed the admission that they were doing so.

(4) With few exceptions they fell victim to the dominance of their sectional cultures. Southern Disciples fought for the Confederacy, Northern Disciples fought for the Union, Disciples in the border states espoused neutrality and even pacifism, and all rationalized their position by proof-texting Scripture. An unconscious adaptation to the presuppositions of the surrounding culture shaped the mind of most Disciples far more than did any careful exposition of either Scripture or the Constitution.[23]

In later generations too many of them subordinated both the biblical witness and the guarantees of the Bill of Rights to the prejudices of the old white Anglo-Saxon Protestant strain in its neurotic reaction to the increasing pluralism of American life. It would be false and unjust to imply that the movement as a whole fell into such a trap. But it must be confessed that Disciples provided a considerable corps of leaders for the Ku Klux Klan in the 1920s (as well as some outspoken opposition) and the founder of the so-called Christian Crusade against Com-

28

munism in the 1950s. The close identification of early Disciples with the American experiment in freedom did not preserve all of their spiritual children from joining movements of demagoguery, repression, and even terror.[24]

Nevertheless, that early love of the Disciples for political and religious freedom cannot fail to impress us when we consider the rise of the movement. In various ways, the many religious types in the United States, from Latter Day Saints to Roman Catholics, incorporated elements from the American commitment to liberty into the shaping of their denominational institutions. For good and for ill, their zeal for the nation and its ideals mingled with their love for Christ and his kingdom. But, aside from the blindness to slavery, the literature of the early Disciples reveals an intense dedication to the idea of liberty both in the state and in the church and a conviction of an authentic relation between the two.

The Coming of Walter Scott

In 1818 a young Scotsman who had studied at the University of Edinburgh immigrated to the United States. Lured by glowing reports of the West, Walter Scott set out the next spring to walk from New York to Pittsburgh. There he fell in with a group of simple Bible Christians popularly dubbed Kissing Baptists. So began that spiritual pilgrimage which would lead him to association with the Campbells and to impressive evangelistic triumphs. It was the preaching of Walter Scott that first won thousands to the position of the Disciples.[25]

Like Campbell, Scott proclaimed an American millennium and saw the divine purpose coming to fulfilment in the emergence of the new nation:

In the United States the two forms of liberty, the political and the religious, are, it is confessed, well defined, and, as we trust, permanently established. The internal and external, the civil and religious, the government of Caesar and the government of God, have each found its proper basis in our country, the one in the Bible, the other in the general constitution, and both in the public consciousness. Thus the two great interests intended to conserve and defend both soul and body are enjoyed here in perfection.

Contemplation of the national heritage and destiny moved Scott to that emotional eloquence for which he was noted:

The landing of the pilgrims on Plymouth rock; the romance of James river and Pocahontas; the joys and sorrows of the first settlers of our country; their successes and reverses, their man-

29

ners and customs, their religious peculiarities and new modes of government, all participate in the spirit of wonder and sweet poesy; and tend to produce in the mind a spirit of glory and heroism that constitute a proper halo in which to enshrine the later and maturer colonial, revolutionary, and national history of "our dear, our native land." If to a history wonderful from the beginning, replete with grand enterprises, and sown broadcast with illustrious events, we add the lofty probability that the whole continent was hid up of God for the future glory of his Son and his people, which people we are, then the permanency and perpetuity of our union follows as a necessity.

Troubled by the swelling wave of Catholic immigration, he nevertheless foresaw Great Britain and America, by their devotion to the Bible and the example of their free institutions inspiring the people of nation after nation "to see and appreciate their own rights and freedom."[26]

Servants of Liberty in the Political Arena

Despite their lyrical commitment to American liberties, early Disciples did not romanticize involvement in the political process. Persons among them endowed with gifts for leadership inclined rather to the direct service of the gospel as of prior importance. John T. Johnson of Kentucky is a good example. A legislator, an officer in the War of 1812, and a member of Congress, he abandoned his political career when he accepted the position of the Disciples. Now he directed his talents to evangelism and to effecting union between the followers of Stone and those of Campbell. Remaining a Baptist and a politician, his brother Richard was elected vice president in 1836 on the Democratic ticket with Martin Van Buren. But Alexander Campbell clearly stated his priorities:

How inferior is the glory of the Honorable Richard M. Johnson, vice-president of this great nation, compared with his brother, the humble servant of Jesus Christ, the most successful proclaimer of the gospel in the great valley of the Mississippi.

Campbell's sentiment is in keeping with that of an inscription commemorating one of the pioneers at Cane Ridge:

Here lies

Nathaniel Rogers—Born July 23, 1755

He was a member of the convention that framed the

Constitution of Kentucky in 1799. What is of far more consequence, he was a member of the Church of Christ in the bosom of which he died, December 22, 1801 at the age of 46, and reposes in the midst of his friends he loved so well.[27]

Some Disciples (like David Lipscomb) carried the priority of Christian loyalty to the point of abstaining on principle from any participation in civil government. Others (like James A. Garfield) entered actively on political careers. Most stood somewhere in between. They rejoiced in their freedom and carried their responsibility as citizens, but for the sake of the good cause they tried to avoid the passions aroused over public issues. Leadership in a constitutional convention debating principles of government seemed appropriate—for Alexander Campbell in Virginia in 1829 as for Winfred Ernest Garrison in New Mexico in 1910. But in the first generation, as the fever of sectionalism rose higher, Disciples remembered their overriding commitment to unity. Hence they were leery of political controversy. Not just on the issue of slavery, but as a rule of life, Campbell sought to preserve "a strict neutrality between party politics, both in . . . oral and written addresses on all subjects."[28]

Disciples in Public Office

As time passed the movement outgrew its early messianism so characteristic of new religious sects. As it won a larger acceptance on the American scene, more Disciples began to seek political office. In the second generation a number gained positions as legislators, governors, and members of Congress. In state politics several gifted women campaigned for prohibition and for women's suffrage; three of these belonged to one congregation in Indianapolis—Annie Holton Dye (mother of Mrs. W. E. Garrison), Emma Eaton White, and Zerelda G. Sanders Wallace (mother of the novelist Lew Wallace). In Kansas a more colorful Disciple, Carry Nation, gained wide celebrity.[29]

In the late nineteenth century and after, political involvement of Disciples continued. On the national scene Thomas W. Phillips, Sr. of Pennsylvania served for a time in Congress. Champ Clark of Missouri was longtime Speaker of the House of Representatives. Alben W. Barkley of Kentucky was Senator and a particularly popular vice president—the "Veep." J. W. Fulbright of Arkansas, serving first in the House and then in the Senate, secured legislation of major importance for international understanding and cultural exchange. Edith Green of Oregon served in the Congress for twenty years. Ronald Reagan of California narrowly missed the Republican nomination for president, and Charles Kirbo, a Georgia lawyer, was Jimmy Carter's personal advisor.

In the diplomatic service the eloquent preacher, Z. T. Sweeney, served as Consul-General to Turkey from 1889 to 1893, and E. T. Williams who had gone to China under the Foreign Christian Missionary Society joined the staff of the American legation to begin a distinguished career as a diplomat and Orientalist. A few Disciples rose to high rank in the military services notably General Omar N. Bradley and General Maxwell Taylor. Clarence Kelley, chief of police in Kansas City became director of the Federal Bureau of Investigation in 1973.[30]

Before the Civil War the most eminent Disciple in public life was Jeremiah Sullivan Black of Pennsylvania whom President Buchanan appointed Attorney General in 1857. (Through Black's good offices Alexander Campbell was presented to the president of the United States.) He became a key figure during the constitutional crisis precipitated by the secession of South Carolina from the Union. Exegeting the Constitution with great care he advised the president that he had no authority to use troops against the secessionists, nor could Congress declare war against a state. As the crisis deepened, the logic of the situation moved Black toward a harder line, but the change of administration in 1861 left the issue up to Abraham Lincoln. In the waning months of his administration, President Buchanan nominated Black to the Supreme Court, but the Senate failed to act. Five years later Black gave the most famous speech of his career, defending before the Supreme Court (*ex parte* Milligan) the right of trial by jury. Later another Disciple, Joseph Rucker Lamar, son of a famous minister, won appointment to the Court.[31]

The careers and utterances of all these persons in public life provide material for the thinking of Disciples on the meaning of liberty. To make that subject manageable in the time at hand, we shall look briefly at presidents of the United States who came from Disciple roots.

Disciples in the White House

More than one religious body has laid claim to Abraham Lincoln. A heavy crop of legends recounts his secret conversion to this or that church. According to one of these—told by Disciples, of course—he came by night to John O'Kane, state evangelist for the Christian Church in Illinois, and was immersed in the Sangamon River. The evidence for these tales is dubious. We do know that Thomas and Sally Lincoln, while they lived in

Indiana, held membership in the Little Pigeon Creek Baptist Church. After their move to Illinois in 1830 they joined a Christian Church. Young Abe Lincoln, 21 years old when the family went West, listened to Disciples and to quite a few other varieties in the prairie pulpits. His repertoire of droll stories included one about a Campbellite preacher with a gift for exaggeration. But the doctrinal disputes of the denominations did not appeal to him. His words have been often quoted:

When any church will inscribe over its altars, as its sole qualification for membership, the Savior's condensed statement of the substance of both law and gospel, "Thou shalt love the Lord thy God with all thy heart, and with all thy soul, and with all thy mind, and thy neighbor as thyself," that church will I join with all my heart and soul.

Disciples surely contributed, along with others, to the religious faith, love for the Bible, and spiritual vision of the Great Emancipator, but no more than any other denomination in his time did they seem to offer the kind of church he sought. Two generations later, however, at University Church of Disciples in Chicago, Edward Scribner Ames placed a bust of Lincoln beside the pulpit and welcomed him into fellowship on the basis of the very qualifications he had espoused.[32]

(Two Disciples of our own time contributed significantly to the collection of Lincolnia and wrote recognized books about the president. Edgar DeWitt Jones spent his early ministry in Kentucky and Illinois. He wrote and lectured eloquently about Lincoln; his great collection is now housed in the Detroit Public Library. Louis A. Warren as a young minister in Hodgenville, Kentucky, began a lifetime of research and writing. Until his retirement he was curator of the Lincoln collection belonging to the Lincoln Life Insurance Company of Fort Wayne, Indiana. Dr. Warren was president of the Disciples of Christ Historical Society in 1957. Dr. Jones' desk now does duty in the office of the Society's president.)[33]

James A. Garfield was a Disciple to the bone. Beginning his public career as a teacher and evangelist, he served as principal of Western Reserve Eclectic Institute (now Hiram College) in Ohio. An ardent foe of slavery and a Unionist, he raised a regiment of volunteers and came out of the Civil War a major general. As Congressman and President he faithfully attended the Vermont Avenue Christian Church in Washington. His Inaugural Address in 1881 included a stirring rhetoric of liberty, but the promise of his presidency was shattered soon after, to remain a haunting memory for those who had loved him. After the shock of his assassination, leading preachers of the

Disciples had the chief roles in the ceremonies of national mourning.

Among his friends and admirers Garfield inspired intense loyalty and extravagant testimonies to his greatness. He evidently possessed a largeness and independence of mind which made him one of the first Disciples of influence to break out of the rigid orthodoxy which had so soon encrusted the thinking of the movement. His rapid rise in the army and in the Republican Party suggests impressive ability and a large quotient of that quality which political observers now call charisma. Not all Disciples admired his political attainments, however, and the Southern pacifists openly criticized his military career. David Lipscomb never ceased to believe that in abandoning the ministry of the gospel, even for the presidency, Garfield had come down to lower ground.

Garfield's opportunity to contribute significantly to the cause of liberty as president was cut short. Only his eloquence on its behalf remains.[34] A good example is the speech which he made in Congress in January, 1865, on the verge of the adoption of the Thirteenth Amendment.

In framing and establishing the Constitution, what restrictions were laid upon the people? Absolutely no human power beyond themselves. No barriers confined them but the laws of nature, the laws of God, their love of justice, and their aspirations for liberty. Over that limitless expanse they ranged at will, and out of such materials as their wisdom selected they built the stately fabric of our Government. That Constitution, with its amendments, is the latest and greatest utterance of American sovereignty. The hour is now at hand when that majestic sovereign, for the benignant purpose of securing still further the "blessings of liberty," is about to put forth another oracle; is about to declare that universal freedom shall be the supreme law of the land. Show me the power that is authorized to forbid it.

Fifteen years later he spoke at the Republican National Convention in Chicago to nominate John Sherman of Ohio as the party's candidate for president. The nomination eventually went to Garfield, in part at least because of the impression made by that oration. It was charged with great emotional power, especially in the "words of peace" which he put on the lips of the personified nation addressing the Confederacy in defeat:

This is our only revenge—that you join us in lifting into the serene firmament of the Constitution, to shine like stars for ever and ever, the immortal principles of truth and justice: that all men, white or black, shall be free, and shall stand equal before the law.

Perhaps Garfield's best known utterance is the line he spoke in New York when the news came of Lincoln's death: "God reigns, and the government at Washington still lives!"

More than eighty years passed before another Disciple came to the White House, ironically as the result of another assassination. Lyndon Baines Johnson, referring to his grandfathers, called himself "a cross between a Baptist preacher and a cowboy." But he was converted and baptized by a Christian preacher. During his presidency he was an honorary elder in National City Christian Church. He maintained a close relationship with his pastor. He graciously accepted a citation from the Disciples of Christ Historical Society.

Caught in the surge of intense popular emotion which repudiated the war in Southeast Asia, Johnson left the nation's highest office under a cloud of disfavor. In the memory of many that cloud still unjustly obscures his massive service to the extension of freedom. For at the beginning of his presidency he threw all the persuasive powers of his personality and his office into the struggle to pass the Civil Rights Act of 1964. The next year he addressed a joint session of Congress in support of the Voting Rights Act: "I speak tonight for the dignity of man and the destiny of democracy." At the end of that speech he raised his arms while quoting three words of the old spiritual that had become a marching song: "We shall overcome." In that moment members of Congress, the visitors in the galleries, and Americans at their television sets across the land wept in high commitment. The passage of these two acts constitutes the largest contribution of any Disciple in the story of American liberty.[35]

"The Pen is Mightier. . ."

Even smaller than the company of Disciples who held high public office was an elect group of brilliant persons who served the cause of liberty in intellectual circles. Giving careful thought both to theory of government and to current issues, they exerted significant influence on public policy.

Most eminent of these in the nineteenth century was Burke Aaron Hinsdale. A student under Garfield, he soon returned to Hiram as a teacher and in 1870 was made president of the college. After twelve years there he became superintendent of schools in Cleveland. In 1888 he went to the University of Michigan as professor of the science and art of teaching, finding release at last from administrative burdens which had long weighed upon him. As prolific an author as Disciples have produced, he wrote on educational theory and method, on history, government, politics, and religion; he also edited *The Works of James Abram Garfield.* For almost a quarter of a century the two men conducted an animated correspondence, hinging on but by no means limited to a ceremonial exchange of letters on New Year's Day. Beginning in 1857, when Hinsdale was only 19, and Garfield 25, and continuing into the brief weeks of the latter's active presidency, the letters reveal a friendship of remarkable intellectual dimension.

With a keen grasp both of the principles of government and of political reality, Hinsdale restrained himself from abstract discussions. His letters say almost nothing of political theory, but its presuppositions underlie much that he writes. In perhaps the most interesting passages he chides Garfield as the Republican leader in Congress for yielding to the politician's love of exaggeration.

I have often noticed in your extemporaneous speeches an excessive use of intensive expressions. "Absolute" seems to be an especial favorite. . . . I am sure . . . that your work as a "stumper" tells upon your habits of discussion and upon the whole tone of your mind, in a way of which you are not aware.

Garfield accepted the detailed criticisms with good grace, defending only some of the usages which Hinsdale had questioned, and the younger man later changed his opinion of one of the speeches in question.[36]

Later when Hinsdale published his work on *The American Government,* he demonstrated the kind of restraint he had commended. He lucidly expounded the way government works under the Constitution, but the book is almost totally devoid of political theory, much less patriotic rhetoric. One of the rare expressions of opinion comes at the very end.

Perhaps there is no government in the world that is more difficult to explain intelligently, and particularly to foreigners, than the American Government. John Quincy Adams called it a "complicated machine; it is an anomaly," said he. . . . No other government is so highly specialized. It combines the complexities of both the dual and the republican systems. But complexity of governmental machinery appears to be essential to liberty.

Hinsdale was the quintessential professor who relied on understatement to serve the cause of freedom.[37]

In 1908 a young minister named Charles Clayton Morrison bought at a sheriff's sale the dubious assets of a small Disciple-oriented journal—its list of subscribers and its name. In scarcely more than a decade he made the *Christian Century* into an international and interdenominational influence. His most dramatic triumph came in his passionate crusade for the outlawry of war. When the representatives of the high contracting powers gathered in 1928 to inscribe their signatures to the Pact of Paris, outlawing war as an instrument of national policy, Morrison was present as an honored guest. The tragic turn of world events in the next decade proved those efforts unavailing, but Morrison continued to contend for freedom on other fronts. His was one of the most articulate voices defending and interpreting the constitutional guarantee of religious liberty. He wrote and spoke widely on the place of religion in public education: it was proper for the public school to teach *about* religion, not to inculcate religious devotion. Opposed to tax support for parochial schools and to the appointment of an ambassador to the Vatican, he led in the formation of the organization now called Americans United for Separation of Church and State. While he attained his greatest fame as an ecumenist, his editorials, books, and speeches on religious liberty reached a wide audience. Eloquently he presented his ideal of a free church standing beside a free state within a free society.[38]

Morrison's colleagues on the *Christian Century* shared his commitment to liberty. W. E. Garrison, church historian and literary editor, wrote consistently on this theme. The titles of several books indicate his concern—*Catholicism and the American Mind* (1928), *Intolerance* (1934), *Faith of the Free* (1940), *Religion and Civil Liberty in the Roman Catholic Tradition* (1946)—as do the passion and insight of his authoritative reviews of major works by others bearing on this theme.[39] Harold E. Fey also championed the cause of freedom with penetrating analyses of trends in American life. He wrote frequent articles and editorials on the rights of the first Americans and has received a citation of honor from the American Indian Congress. He was ever alert to any threat to freedom of speech, press, or religion.[40] The ecumenical commitment of all three of these editors served the ideal of a united church unreservedly committed to civil and religious liberty.

One other Disciple deserves a place in this company. A quiet and meticulous scholar, M. Searle Bates served as a missionary in China from 1920 to 1950. He was professor of history in the University of Nanking, then for a quarter of a century was professor of missions at Union Theological Seminary in New York. In 1942 he was appointed to the staff of a joint committee of the Foreign Missions Conference of North America and the

37

Federal Council of the Churches of Christ in America to investigate problems of religious freedom around the world. His book growing out of that study appeared under the title *Religious Liberty: An Inquiry.* A magisterial survey, it presents case studies in particular problems, a historical overview, a theoretical and legal analysis, and a careful set of conclusions.

Appearing just as World War II came to its end, the book was both relevant and timely. Treaties of peace were being written, new nations were drafting constitutions, and the United Nations was struggling to formulate its Declaration of Human Rights. Ecumenical leaders in Asia, Europe, and America were pleading the cause of religious liberty.

Translations of the book were announced in more than half a dozen languages. The edition in English quickly sold out and a second printing was ordered, with five hundred copies being sent to India for presentation to members of the first Constituent Assembly, government officials, and university libraries. India's Constitution of 1950 acknowledged the right "freely to profess, practice and propagate religion," and the report of the Foreign Missions Conference for that year claimed that the book undoubtedly influenced these liberal provisions. While specific influences on a document issuing from a political assembly are manifold and complex, this study was the definitive work on religious liberty in a time of decision in many parts of the world.

As for Searle Bates, on the day he finished reading proofs, he sailed again for Australia, India, and China. Not till eighteen months after publication did he see a copy of his book, "carried by yak over the great mountains from India to China." We may safely say that no other Disciple has had so large an influence on the charters of human liberty.[41]

Celebrators of Freedom

Disciples regard themselves as a highly rational people in the religious world, given more to sober reflection and common-sense argument than to emotional expression. Their relatively small contribution to the hymnody of the church seems to substantiate this impression. Yet by a strange paradox the best known contributions of Disciples in the field of liberty have come not from their intellectual theorists but from their artists, preachers, and poets. We should not be surprised, for as an expression of the human spirit art flourishes as a venture in freedom.[42]

38

The Artists

One of the clichés of this year's Bicentennial observance of the American Revolution is the painting, "The Spirit of '76" by Archibald Willard. Its story has been graphically told by Henry K. Shaw. Willard was a cartoonist and artist in Ohio, who enjoyed considerable popularity a century ago. As the nation's centennial drew on, an art dealer named Ryder asked him to work up a picture that would catch the spirit of the celebration. Willard began toying with a humorous sketch of men marching with fife and drum after a drink or two in a patriotic parade. He thought he would call the picture "Yankee Doodle." About that time the artist's father, Samuel Willard died. Giving "serious thought" to his father's life and death and the deeper meaning of the national anniversary, Willard went to his canvas to produce a more sublime rendition of his theme. So the well loved painting came forth, the procession of ragged Continentals led by a strong, white-haired veteran rolling his drum for liberty. In the picture he appears as an old soldier of the War for Independence. But the face is that of the artist's father—a preacher of the Disciples who established and cared for churches across a lifetime of ministry and who loved his country.

First acclaimed for bronzes shown at the World's Columbian Exposition in Chicago in 1893, Alexander Phimister Proctor, a celebrated sculptor, won distinguished commissions for half a century. His statuary represents wild animals of the West, Indians, and various national heroes. He did a commemorative placque for the stations of the Pony Express; the *Pioneer* at the University of Oregon; *The Circuit Rider* at Salem; and two complimentary statues of *The Pioneer Mother;* one, a figure in Kansas City, idealizes a young woman on horseback, holding a baby and pressing westward. The other figure in Eugene, Oregon, depicts an older woman, seated in dignified and well earned repose at the end of the trail. His last great piece, entitled *Mustangs*, stands at the University of Texas.

When young Proctor left Colorado in 1885 to study in the East he carried a letter from his friend Bayard Craig, pastor of Central Christian Church in Denver, to B. B. Tyler, distinguished Disciple minister in New York. He formed a friendship with the Tyler family and took membership with the Christian Church on Sixty-Sixth Street. The love of freedom marks his works.[43]

When the Disciples of Christ Historical Society erected its building, the Thomas W. Phillips Memorial in Nashville, a Fine Arts Committee selected themes for artistic treatment. Stained glass executed by Nashville artist Gus Baker for the conference room celebrates unity and liberty in Christ. Windows in the lecture hall honor champions of civil and religious liberty, and others elsewhere symbolize further aspects of freedom.[44] Stone shields sculpted by Puryear Mims of Nashville include representations of meetinghouse, college, printing press, circuit rider, and Conestoga wagon, honoring those pioneers

Whose stern, impassioned stress
A thoroughfare for freedom beat
Across the wilderness!

The Preachers

By the end of the nineteenth century, Disciples had developed an urban ministry led by preachers of impressiveness and influence. I include them here among the artistic types who celebrated the values cherished by American Christians, for that is where they belong. They lived in the era of Romanticism. Unlike the founding generation, they were not so much polemicists as interpreters; unlike our contemporary clergymen, not so much administrators as orators. As pastors of sizeable churches, they held an important place in the life of their communities. Frequently they gave voice to the nation's commitments to liberty, linking these with their understanding of the gospel. Some such utterances cross the border into civil religion. Some too easily accept the *status quo*. Yet typically they voice a devotion to freedom derived from and harmonious with their Christian allegiance.

In the third year of the present century, E. L. Powell of Louisville issued a book of "Addresses on Civic Righteousness." In one of these he said,

There is . . . a liberty which no government can confer, the liberty of righteousness, which comes about through Christ, who sets the soul free from the power and dominion of evil. This liberty must be wrought out by the individual under the guidance of him who said: "Ye shall know the truth, and the truth shall make you free." But the just government will provide that environment of law and political condition which makes it possible for the individual man, without molestation, to develop himself to the highest degree. He must have liberty to think, and hence government must permit no censorship or inquisition. He must have liberty of religion, and hence there can be no discrimination against any religion that shows itself to be a religion within the definition of the term. He must have liberty of person within the limitations of protection to the community and hence, foreign or home oppression must be resented. Liberty, within the scope

of the great truth—"The greatest good of the greatest number."
Priceless blessing, indeed! . . . But we are, as yet, far from the
attainment of the ideal.[45]

Frederick D. Kershner was an eminent intellectual of the
theological center among Disciples in the first half of the twentieth century. He served successively as editor of *The Chris-*
tian-Evangelist and the *Christian Standard,* then at three universities, Texas Christian, Drake, and Butler. A theologian of
broad learning, he was also a popular preacher. His book of
Sermons for Special Days contains addresses for the birthdays
of Washington and Lincoln, Decoration Day, Flag Day, Independence Day, Labor Day, and Thanksgiving; these pieces for
patriotic occasions exceed those for the high liturgical seasons.
The book vividly exemplifies the way in which, only half a
century ago, the calendar of civil religion contributed more to
the structure of ceremonial life in many churches than did the
Christian year (only recently discovered by Disciples). Yet
Kershner was a responsible theologian. While his utterances
express patriotic sentiment, it is held within a higher Christian
allegiance:

There is a petty loyalty which does not think of higher things;
which says "my country, right or wrong," instead of saying, as
it should, "my country, to be followed when right, and to be set
right when wrong."
. . . . The ultimate and final loyalty of any human being must be
to his ultimate and final ideal which means, of course, his God.[46]

Perhaps no preacher of the Disciples spoke to more people in
the twentieth century than the evangelist Charles Reign Scoville. Preaching on "The Purpose of the Ages" he interpreted
divine Providence throughout history until he came to the
founding of the American nation:

Here, as nowhere else on the whole earth's surface or in the whole
world's history, could a fiat go forth, proclaiming the inalienable
rights of man, the freedom and equality of the masses, and the
kingship of the common people. And here as nowhere else the
intellect has a free school, unhampered by church or govern-
ment; the heart a free church, not dominated by priest or pope,
school or state; and the will of a free government; "of the people,
by the people, and for the people." Here the king does not own the
people, but the people own the king. The greatest ruler must
become the greatest servant, and the chief ruler become the chief
servant. In this we are following Him who was Creator of all,
and yet who became the Servant of all. . . . All men were declared
free and equal. Think of it! Liberty and coronation, the downfall

of despotism and the enthroning of common men! A government of the people, for the people, and by the people! A movement that shattered thrones and moves the world.[47]

Edgar DeWitt Jones, who has already been mentioned, loved the great orators of the American past, not only the preachers but the political leaders as well. These he celebrated in a book he called *Lords of Speech*. Through the years he delivered many sermons and addresses which lifted up the ideals of the nation. One of these, "The American Dream," he concluded with a stirring paraphrase on the eleventh chapter of Hebrews. A single paragraph runs,

By faith Thomas Jefferson was stirred to strike a blow for political independence and wrote the thrilling document that declared that all men are created equal and endowed with certain inalienable rights. By faith he said, "Love your neighbor as yourself and your country more than yourself."

He delivered many orations on the Great Emancipator, with a special fondness for his prize-winning sermon, "The Greatening of Abraham Lincoln."[48]

Other preachers beyond counting spoke of freedom, not merely to stir patriotic emotion but to deepen understanding of the nation's venture in liberty. Most of those who published their utterances held their democratic ethos and their Christian devotion very close together without compromising the claims of Christ as Lord. Their spirit is well summed up in a pledge which Charles S. Medbury of Des Moines wrote for his ministry:

To this day that is mine, my country's and my God's, I dedicate my all. My talents, every one, shall be held subject to the sight draft of the emergencies of others. I will enlarge my soul by cultivating love for those from whom I find myself recoiling. No man shall ever feel his color or his caste in my presence, for within my heart of hearts there shall be no consciousness of it.

. . . .

. . . Help me, Thou whose manger cradle brought democracy to light, to meet in my own worth democracy's final test and to my own great day to be true.[49]

The Poets

The first generation of poets who sang the ideals of the new nation lived for the most part in New England, without a Disciple among them. But just at the turn of twentieth century a new company of bards emerged to compose the songs of a liberty-loving people. Slightly out of fashion in our bruised and cynical decade, they nevertheless stirred the hearts of thousands with their celebration of the democratic faith. Two of these were Disciples.

In northern California young Edwin Markham, tending sheep in the Suisun Hills, committed to memory pages of the Gospels. He listened to his mother's verses and the sermons of the Christian preachers and was immersed in a deep pool near San Jose. He attended Christian College in Santa Rosa. Though he later joined another church he retained his affection for the Disciples, in "those early days, perhaps . . . the best read persons in Bible lore." Like Lindsay, he wrote a memorable poem on Lincoln. But his most powerful and influential piece was inspired by seeing Millet's famous painting, "The Man With The Hoe." Moved by the artist's fatalistic but faithful depiction of the unknown peasant brutalized by exploitation Markham uttered a cry heard round the world. His "Man With The Hoe" is an impassioned call for human dignity and justice, for liberty both political and economic. He believed so profoundly in the right of freedom that he foretold the inevitability of revolution wherever oppressive systems should undertake to deny human rights.

> Is this the Thing the Lord God made and gave
> To have dominion over sea and land;
> To trace the stars and search the heavens for power;
> To feel the passion of Eternity?
> Is this the dream He dreamed who shaped the suns
> And marked their ways upon the ancient deep?
> . . . .
>
> O masters, lords and rulers in all lands,
> Is this the handiwork you give to God,
> This monstrous thing distorted and soul-quenched?
> How will you ever straighten up this shape;
> Touch it again with immortality;
> Give back the upward looking and the light;
> Rebuild in it the music and the dream;
> Make right the immemorial infamies,
> Perfidious wrongs, immedicable woes?
> How answer his brute question in that hour
> When whirlwinds and rebellions shake all shores?
> How will it be with kingdoms and with kings—
> With those who shaped him to the thing he is—
> When this dumb terror shall rise to judge the world,
> After the silence of the centuries?[50]

Less prophetic in style but equally religious was Vachel Lindsay of Illinois. The grandson of an Indiana farmer-preacher ("His was an ironside, democratic pride"), the boy grew up in Springfield in an atmosphere redolent with memories of Lincoln. Composing his verse to the exuberant rhythms of cakewalk, spirituals, and jazz, he celebrated the rambunctious faith of the people he loved. He wrote of countryside and village and city, of Jackson and Lincoln and Bryan, of oldtime preachers like Peter Jackson and Alexander Campbell and his Grandfather Frazee, of the Salvation Army and the world missionary crusade, and again and again of the love of freedom. He deserves a whole lecture in himself.

Lindsay's millenial, libertarian spirit comes through most compellingly in his rollicking poems on the folk-heroes of the West. Here are a few lines from "In Praise of Johnny Appleseed."

> Washington buried in Virginia,
> Jackson buried in Tennessee,
> Young Lincoln, brooding in Illinois,
> And Johnny Appleseed, priestly and free,
> Knotted and gnarled, past seventy years,
> Still planted on in the woods alone.
>
> ....
>
> An angel in each apple that touched the forest mold,
> A ballot-box in each apple,
> A state capital in each apple,
> Great high schools, great colleges,
> All America in each apple. . . .[51]

No other Disciple approached Markham and Lindsay in stature as a poet. Mention must be made, however, of Thomas Curtis Clark, whose inspirational verse appearing in *The Christian Century* for a generation sang of a liberal faith committed to social justice. Typical is "The Faith of Christ's Freemen."

> God was and is and e'er shall be;
>   Christ lived and loved—and loves us still;
> And man goes forward, proud and free,
>   God's present purpose to fulfill.[52]

The Disciples' Devotion to Political Liberty

Disciples of Christ took their rise on the frontier of the young nation and pursued their freedom-lovers' vision of the church

44

while participating fully in the developing life of the United States. For all their high intent to restore primitive Christianity, theirs was a highly acculturated form of faith, an *American* religious movement. Not uncommonly at the Lord's table I have heard elders give thanks in successive sentences for this free land where we may worship according to the dictates of our own conscience and for these emblems of our Savior's body and blood. The words of the preachers and the poets have often celebrated the same comfortable coexistence between love for the nation's commitment to liberty and love for God the giver of all good things. American Christians, Disciples included, have made the combination so readily because they have perceived God as Author of Liberty and their country as the land of the free. Although the popular attitude often seems uncritical, we must acknowledge that Disciples have clearly declared God to be transcendent over the nation. The preachers we have quoted retained an unclouded perception of divine sovereignty. Editors and missionaries called political leaders to account for policies which threatened the liberties of Americans or trampled on the liberties of others.

The democratic ethos of American Disciples presents an instructive paradox. On the one hand, their devotion to the ideals of freedom is of the essence of their spirit, inseparable from their Christian faith. On the other hand, in this characteristic they appear in no sense unique among religious groups in the United States. Whatever Disciples have brought to the altar of political liberty has come, not from the distinctive spiritual estates of Stone and the Campbells, but from the common heritage of all Americans. As advocates of freedom, Disciples have stood with free spirits from many traditions, religious and humane, and in service to a common cause all these have found themselves one. Perhaps this is the genius of Disciples after all, in politics as well as in the ecclesiastical sphere: to concentrate on the essentials which unite.

In any case, Disciples have loved freedom. And when they have spoken of the national destiny, or even of human nature, they have like other Americans used the vocabulary of religion. Their democratic faith and their Christian confession have lived together in intimate union, each inspiring and vivifying the other. Look a genuine Disciple in the eye and you will discern there what Vachel Lindsay saw in the portrait of Alexander Campbell: . . . "that air of going on, forever free."[53]

2. Liberating the Human Spirit

Some Personal Dimensions of Freedom

You shall know the truth: and the truth shall make you free
—*John 8:32*

For nearly a century and a half of the nation's independence, most Americans talked of freedom in political language. They honored the Constitution of the United States and fervently professed their love for the land of the free. In the past half century the point of pressure has shifted. At least since the Lost Generation and the rebelliousness of Flaming Youth in the 1920s, the opinion-makers have seen the struggle for liberty in more personal terms. The quest has become as much existential as political, an issue to be fought out in each person's life. This shift to the personal does not represent an abrupt break with the past; rather it is a matter of emphasis. We need only recall Thoreau in the early nineteenth century to encounter a man occupied with freedom in its existential aspects or remember the civil rights movement of the 1960s to know that political concern continued.

The reason for the shift is not hard to see. After the Civil War technological change overtook agrarian America. Our population moved to the cities, and persons got lost in the crowd. The magnitudes of economic power increased with each passing decade. Millions of sensitive persons felt themselves molded by the system, trapped within the system, crushed by the system. They began to search for personal identity, to crusade for the assertion of personal integrity, to try their hand at taming and humanizing the system itself.

Disciples of Christ participated enthusiastically, if typically, in the American experiment with political freedom. They have no disposition to abandon that venture. But as the front has shifted to more personal or existential ground we may well ask what part Disciples have played. That inquiry becomes the focus of this lecture.

Again I disavow any intention of trying to prove the Disciples unique or even foremost in the struggle for liberty. But as a sample of Christian thought and experience in middle America, this particular slice of church life illustrates important aspects of the quest for personal freedom. To gain historical understanding in religion we need to concern ourselves not so much with institutions as with motivation. What have believers done in the life of society? What made them behave as they did, not primarily in church but in the crucial struggles that affect human destiny? With such questions in mind, we consider Disciples of Christ and the liberation of the human spirit.[1]

Free Spirits among the Disciples

One way of getting into the topic is to reflect on the question: Who among the Disciples has been most truly free? Once that query has been put, a gallery of fascinating personalities flashes on the screen of our imaginations. Let me suggest a few of these free spirits.

See young Walter Scott tramping with elation through majestic Appalachian forests on the trail from New York to Pittsburgh, reveling in continental wonders which surpass all previous imagination.[2]

Watch that entire congregation of Disciples, with Davy Crockett as guide, moving from Tennessee to Texas—Crockett in his coonskin cap, rejoicing in his mastery of the wilderness, boasting of his prowess in killing 105 bears on one hunting spree, hurrying on in advance of the caravan to defend the Alamo; and the "church on wheels and on horseback" proceeding more deliberately but no less determinedly, to settle in that far land. One person in that train is young Hetty D'Spain. Her sons, born in this new country, will lay the foundations for Texas Christian University.[3]

Look at young Peter H. Burnett, promising member of a prominent Disciple family, who went out the Oregon Trail in 1843. On Christmas at Fort Vancouver he found his soul thrilled by the "profound solemnity" of the midnight mass. Borrowing a copy of the Campbell-Purcell debate from a Baptist preacher, he concluded that "On many points . . . Mr. Campbell had been overthrown." Over the next eighteen months he read everything he could find on Roman Catholicism, praying to "know the truth, and then have the grace to follow wherever it might lead." At last he went to a priest of the "Old Church" for baptism. Then in the Gold Rush he headed south, to become the first governor of the state of California.[4]

Consider Alexander Cross. Born a slave, he responded to the gospel and began to preach among his people with notable effectiveness. The Christian Church at Hopkinsville, Kentucky, purchased his freedom and in 1853 under auspices of the American Christian Missionary Society he sailed for Liberia as a missionary.[5]

Think of Archie Campbell, nephew of Alexander, graduating with highest honors from the College of William and Mary in 1853. The next June the John Robinson Circus played the West Virginia Hills, and young Archie ran off with the show to spend the rest of his life as a clown. Now who hasn't wanted to do that?[6]

Watch Champ Clark, youthful *bon vivant* in Hannibal, Missouri joining a party of young people in a dance on a Mississippi riverboat. On Sunday the congregation meets to exercise discipline and sternly withdraws fellowship from the promising young man. Next Sunday when the gospel is preached and the invitation offered, Champ Clark goes forward. What congregation of Disciples can refuse the right hand of fellowship?[7]

Look at that company of 75 women meeting in Cincinnati in 1874 to form the Christian Woman's Board of Missions and get the Disciples back in the business of worldwide witness when the "leaders" of the brotherhood (the men!) were stymied. Look at little groups of determined women with the same purpose springing up in congregations all over the country; you see the beginnings of a movement that still continues. Look at another little group meeting in St. Louis in 1886 to establish the National Benevolent Association. "They said it couldn't be done," and the women found freedom to do it.[8]

Turn your eyes to the Old West where cowboys roam the range. Out of that tough and lithe company of free spirits rides a young Scot, whose studies at the University of Glasgow once earned him a master's degree before he set out for Texas. One

48

Saturday afternoon in Amarillo, with a few drinks under his belt, H. D. C. Maclachlan pays a call on the Christian preacher, picks up a Greek New Testament, and begins to read. Encouraged by the preacher, he goes to the College of the Bible in Lexington and becomes an eloquent and effective minister, serving for 21 years at Seventh Street Church in Richmond, Virginia. Another Texan who stays on the ranch is Luke Brite, putting together a fortune in cattle and oil and leaving his name on the Divinity School of Texas Christian University. Akin to these two and all the other hard-riding caballeros of the Disciples is the legendary E. F. Boggess, pastor of the Christian Church at Guthrie, Oklahoma in 1893 at the time of the opening of the Cherokee Strip. The Board of Church Extension persuades him to buy a fast horse and enter the run to stake out lots for churches in the new town sites. So he contributes his colorful page to the lore of the Disciples. A decade afterwards the Board of Church Extension conducts a contest for a ballad celebrating Boggess' Ride. It is won by Rose Bush Wilkinson of Hastings, Nebraska and the ballad is read at the 1904 National Convention.

> Here's the train—over-laden—kept at eight-hour speed;
>   There are vehicles varied; wheels vieing with steed,
> And yonder is Boggess away in the lead,
>   On the horse that seems proud of his training.
> See! He leaps a broad stream. 'Tis a full rod across—
>   Then onward he goes, without swerving or pause.
> Oh! well rides our friend for the good of the Cause—
>   The cause so well worth our maintaining.
>
> On—on, see him speed o'er the wide, rolling prairie.
>   On—on, till he reaches the town-site of Perry. . . .

That rider at full gallop is memorialized in stained glass in a window of the Marshall Building at Phillips University in Enid.[9]

Or take a look at a debonair young American *Wheeling through Europe* at the turn of the century, writing up his travels for his father's paper, then putting the pieces together for the first of his many books. Of course, it is W. E. Garrison. He has a line of cycling peers among Disciples. In 1899 a young Swedish immigrant named Victor Hoven, pedaled from Iowa west through Yellowstone Park, then proceeded to Oregon to enroll in Eugene Divinity School where he would spend a lifetime as a teacher. And in this Bicentennial Year Professor Keith Watkins of Christian Theological Seminary and his daughter Sharon bicycled from Portland, Oregon to Indianapolis, 2630 miles in 31 days of riding, just for the fun of doing it.[10]

Other far-roaming spirits come into view. There is Vachel Lindsay vagabonding across the country, piling the "sheaves of glory" in Kansas, trading rhymes for bread (in the original and not the recent colloquial meaning of that word), turning up unannounced at a schoolhouse or college to preach the gospel of beauty. "And we felt free in Kansas from any sort of fear. . . ."[11]

See Abe Cory and Rafe Miller, barn-storming for the Lord in the famous Men and Millions Movement. After three almost fruitless days of soliciting in the Ozarks, these nationally known leaders stand with heads uncovered before the grave of Jesse James, offering their tribute to one who knew how to get money out of these tight-fisted natives.[12]

Look, but not too closely at Sally Rand, rocketing to fame as exponent of a new form of terpsichorean art at the Chicago World's Fair and bringing a touch of excitement to a nation enduring the Great Depression. (I have it on the authority of one of the most dignified and sensitive ladies among the Disciples, whose name all would know, that the act was indeed artistic and done in good taste.) What many have not realized—apparently the reporters failed to discover it—was Sally Rand's practice, while on tour, of hunting up the Christian Church and coming on Sundays to worship inconspicuously with her people.[13]

Watch veteran missionary Royal J. Dye standing with host pastor Orman L. Shelton before the celebrated statue of the Pioneer Mother in Ponca City, Oklahoma. The tears stream down the old doctor's face as he softly whispers, "That's my Mother!" In her we see embodied thousands of Christian women who tramped the trails to the West.[14]

Gaze at the venerable but vigorous A. W. Fortune, one of the most scholarly of ministers, suddenly losing his eyesight at the age of seventy. Within weeks of unsuccessful surgery, he is listening to Talking Books and learning Braille. Soon he is reading and writing as much as ever. Four years later he preaches or lectures seventy-seven times. He leaves nearly a hundred manuscripts in Braille, and keeps to the end the eagerness of a free spirit: "I have learned many things that I would not have known if I had retained my sight, and for these I thank God."[15]

Consider Vivian Kellems, manufacturer in New London, Connecticut, who for years carried on a vigorous fight against the Federal Government contesting tax laws which she said discriminated unjustly against single persons. Even though her estate paid at last, she held out till death.[16]

50

Or look at John Wooden, learning to play basketball in Indiana (where it induces Hoosier Hysteria), winning the state high school championship as a coach, then going West to become a legend at UCLA. In all those years when his teams were ranked Number One, John Wooden remained himself, an unpretentious exemplar of good sportsmanship, an inspiring teacher of youth, an active member of the Christian Church.[17]

In this gallery of free spirits, the thread of personal liberty connects all the portraits. Both in the nineteenth century and in the twentieth, Disciples were born free and born again free, and they never lost their love of liberty.

We turn now to a more systematic consideration of our topic. I intend to explore the Disciples' contribution to liberating the human spirit under two main heads: evangelism and education, then to conclude with a word about certain exemplars of personal freedom.

Evangelism, the Gift of Freedom

In the quest for personal liberation the early Disciple evangelists saw themselves as emancipators of the human spirit. In a time less exposed to pluralism and relativism than our own they confidently offered the gift of interior freedom. If we suppose that only old-time fundamentalists trouble themselves with such concerns nowadays, we do not know our own generation. Consider, for example, the "frantic pilgrimage" which Jerry Rubin describes in his recent autobiography. Before he was out of his thirties he had run through "a smorgasbord course in New Consciousness":

EST, gestalt therapy, bioenergetics, Rolfing, massage, jogging, health foods, t'ai chi ch'uan, Esalen, hypnotism, modern dance, meditation, Silva Mind Control, Arica, acupuncture, sex therapy, Reichian therapy, and More House.

Every few weeks we hear of another brand name in pop psychology or cultic religion to add to such a list. Some of these represent serious and responsible efforts to deal with the human condition; others are obvious gimmickry packaged and rushed to market as bait for thousands, confusedly shopping for personal liberation and hoping to discover "the real Me."[18]

The rapid growth of the Disciples in the nineteenth century and the direct word of many who responded to their preaching indicate that they were addressing a widely felt and powerful interior need. To thousands, their evangelism came as a gift of freedom. It brought liberty to act in the deep realms of the

51

human spirit. It brought deliverance from ignorance and superstition. It offered redemption from sin and death. It promised liberation from an oppressive social system. These notes sound in the preaching of the great evangelists (Walter Scott, Knowles Shaw, John V. Updike, and Charles Reign Scoville) as well as in the proclamation of a host of other preachers.

While the message came in simple terms, remarkably free from the scholastic language of much Christian preaching at the time, it was carefully thought through. The early Disciples were indeed anti-creedal, pouring eloquent scorn on the elaborate theological systems of the various denominations, but they were not anti-intellectual. Rather, as the late Dean W. B. Blakemore observed, "Scott's evangelistic power could not have existed apart from his theological power." What was true of Scott was true of the others also. They offered a sane, scriptural, practical message of salvation. If their preaching was suffused with the emotion of great concern, it was guided by reason which carefully searched the Scriptures and the human heart. And the message came as a liberating word.[19] Let us consider its characteristic notes.

Freedom to Respond to the Gospel

The dominant theology in American Protestantism when Disciples came on the scene was Calvinism. Ever since the Reformation the preachers of that persuasion—Presbyterian, Congregationalist, Reformed, Baptist—had rung the changes on a rigid doctrine of double predestination, divine election to salvation and divine reprobation to eternal punishment, which left the most conscientious person utterly helpless in respect to one's spiritual condition. Those who were consistent taught that it was improper for an unredeemed person even to pray for deliverance since the divine decrees had already determined the outcome from before the foundation of the world. Many persons facing the raw uncertainty of life on the frontier suffered untold anguish as they agonized about their eternal fate. The ordeal of "Raccoon" John Smith in early Kentucky was typical.[20]

The Calvinist theory of an election at once irrational and aristocratic ran into increasing resistance in the egalitarian atmosphere of the new American democracy. Methodists and other avowed Arminians set themselves flatly against it, as did increasing numbers of revivalists from churches in the orthodox tradition. But the rigid doctrine of election had the authority of great names behind it—Calvin, Luther, Augustine, and (it was claimed) the apostle Paul. Those Presbyterians and Baptists who inclined toward softening the position were denounced as heretics. A long time was to pass before these churches tempered their official position.

In such a setting, Walter Scott's discovery of "A Divinely Authorized Plan for Preaching the Christian Religion" came as an epic of personal liberation. By a careful analysis of the conversions in the New Testament he isolated five "steps" in the process of salvation. All followed on hearing the Gospel preached, and all were open to any one who chose to act. They were Faith, Repentance, Baptism, Remission of Sins, Gift of Eternal Life. In time he would call the simple formula "the Gospel Restored." He put it on the five fingers of the hand so that any one could see it and grasp it and act on it: (1) Faith: anyone who listens honestly to the facts about Jesus Christ can believe by accepting the evidence. God has acted to save sinners in the gift of his Son. No one need wait for any special miracle. (2) Repentance: anyone who believes in Jesus Christ can, in response to the gospel, turn from sin to confess Jesus Christ as Savior and Lord. (3) Baptism: the immersion of the penitent believer is "a positive ordinance"—an objective act—open to any penitent believer. (4) Remission of sins: God has promised forgiveness to all who offer themselves sincerely for baptism. No other sign, no inward emotional upheaval, is necessary. (5) Gift of Eternal Life: God has promised the Holy Spirit and Life Everlasting to all who by baptism accept his offer of forgiveness.

In 1827 at New Lisbon, Ohio, Scott presented the "plan of salvation" for the first time from the pulpit and, somewhat to the preacher's surprise, a man named William Amend presented himself in response to the sermon. Scott's biographer later observed that "Mr. Amend was, beyond all question, the first person in modern times who received the ordinance of baptism in perfect accordance with apostolic teaching and usage." Soon thousands of others followed, and the rapid growth of Disciples was under way.

Later generations of Disciples, after Scott's five-finger exercise had itself become a form of legalism, have sometimes lost sight of the liberation which it brought to thousands troubled by the old Calvinism. But to Disciples throughout the nineteenth century it was clearly a word of freedom. "Whosoever will may come" became a characteristic text.

And still in the twentieth century that faith has served as a liberating principle, not only in its immediate reference to accepting the gospel, but more profoundly in establishing basic patterns of personality. In the days of struggle and poverty at the beginning of his career, the eminent contemporary artist Robert Rauschenberg could not share the mood of self-pity so common among his artistic colleagues. As a child he had carried home colored picture cards of Bible stories from the Church of Christ in Port Arthur, Texas. He also took with him something else, which shaped both his personality and his career: "I had the feeling from my early church background that, well, it's you who decided to live this life, and that's the moral choice." Freedom to respond to the gospel both implies and contributes to a larger pattern of freedom.[21]

Freedom from Creedalism

From the outset of the movement, its earliest leaders proclaimed emancipation from creeds and authoritarian confessions of faith. Protestant scholasticism had outdone itself in efforts at precise verbal formulation concerning the fine points of theology, mystifying the laity and dividing the churches. Barton Stone early set himself against certain doctrines of the Westminster Confession which seemed to him contrary to common sense and unwarranted by the Bible. The Last Will and Testament of the Springfield Presbytery declared,

We will, *that the people henceforth take the Bible as the only sure guide to heaven; and as many as are offended with other books, which stand in competition with it, may cast them into the fire if they choose; for it is better to enter into life having one book, than having many to be cast into hell.*

In the same way Thomas Campbell repudiated creeds and confessions in the Declaration and Address.

Although doctrinal exhibitions of the great system of divine truths, and defensive testimonies in opposition to prevailing errors, be highly expedient; and the more full and explicit they be, for those purposes, the better; yet as these must be in a great measure the effect of human reasoning, and of course must contain many inferential truths, they ought not to be made terms of christian communion. . . .

Disciples sought emancipation from the elaborate documents of Protestant confessionalism, which ran to hundreds of pages, and from the ecclesiastical authorities which undertook to enforce adherence to them. President E. V. Zollars of Oklahoma Christian University characterized "The Faith That Saves":

It furnishes a practical way of converting the world, and the only way. In no other way can all classes be reached, but in this way a man can be made a Christian in a single hour, as in the

beginning. It requires months to indoctrinate men in the multi-plied articles of creeds and confessions of faith, but a man may hear the facts, commands and promises of the gospel stated in a single sermon, believe and obey the selfsame hour, and thus be saved.[22]

The early Disciple rejection of creeds implied no formless faith, no exaltation of subjectivism in belief. In their view, Christianity was a revealed religion, but most of the disputed doctrines on which the confessions pronounced in such punctilious detail were not part of the revelation. They were at best, inferences from Scripture.

Against the authority of creeds and confessions Disciples in their quest for Christian freedom set two other tests of orthodoxy. (Let us observe that they did not always interpret the two harmoniously.) These two tests were Holy Scripture (in effect, the New Testament) and the person of Jesus Christ. Two slogans of the middle period indicate their function: "No Book but the Bible" and "No Creed but Christ."

In setting the Bible against the creeds, Disciples appealed to the same ultimate authority in doctrine then acknowledged by all Protestants. But they dismissed as unnecessary and confusing the authoritative confessions or "subordinate standards" by which the various churches had undertaken to systematize biblical doctrine. Disciples saw these as an affront to the dignity of Scripture. If an item of belief was not clearly set forth in the New Testament, the creedal declaration was unjustified; if it was in the Bible, the creed was unnecessary. The Bible alone was sufficient. And even in expounding Scripture, Disciples did not believe that they were holding forth abstract notions as the substance of faith. Rather, in Campbell's words, the Bible was a book of "facts." It recounted deeds done in history. Acceptance of the recorded evidence became (in their Lockean epistemology) a sure and convincing basis for confessing Jesus as the Christ. Many Disciples developed a rigid biblical legalism. Some came to speak of the Bible as the Christian creed, insisting on assent to its every word. But the appeal to Scripture as setting forth the essentials of salvation and the consequent repudiation of creeds and ecclesiastical authorities was an effort at liberation. With the Bible in the hands of the people, they were free to read for themselves the essentials of the faith.

Needless to say, the revolution in the understanding of the Bible which has occurred in America in the twentieth century has altered the basis for doing theology on the part of many Disciples. When we read Alexander Campbell he still impresses us as a man of great amplitude of mind, but some of his presuppositions about Holy Scripture strike us as quaint and untenable.[23]

In focusing on the person of Jesus Christ as the center of Christian faith, Disciples hit on a formula which provided simultaneously power, authority, and freedom for the believer. It helped to overcome the cool rationalism with which they often handled Scripture in the manner of someone working with mathematical equations and warmed their simple faith with the ardor of loyalty to a person. In the words of E. V. Zollars, one "may believe a proposition intellectually, but to believe on a person calls for the exercise of the affections." Customarily, Disciples did not rely on the build-up of intense emotion as a background for conversion, as their Methodist contemporaries (who also rejected Calvinism) tended to do. Disciples preferred to think of the preaching which produced faith as dominantly rational in its appeal, though pervaded with feeling which is a component of conviction. Nevertheless in centering on the person of Jesus Christ the faith incorporated strong emotional attachment. Common loyalty to the one Lord, they held, provided a basis of unity among believers while at the same time leaving them free of the demands for uniformity which Christians have so often imposed on one another. So they rejoiced in "the simplicity that is in Christ" as "the creed that needs no revision," and in the liberation of spirit which they found in him.[24]

Deliverance from Ignorance and Superstition

In ecumenical circles the late George Beazley used to remind his colleagues that the Christian Church (Disciples of Christ) was virtually unique among the major churches in having originated *after* the Enlightenment at a time when the presuppositions of the Age of Reason still enjoyed wide currency. Thus Disciples accorded to rationality and "common sense" an esteem far higher than they commanded in the other "people's churches" which grew so rapidly in the revivalistic atmosphere of the frontier. Furthermore, the prominence of debating in the formative years of the Disciples gave to their preaching a polemical tendency which long endured. Their Methodist rivals put it down as "head religion." If Disciples after Campbell produced no "theologians" until the twentieth century (because of their anti-confessional stance), neither did they promote as a popular religious value that anti-intellectualism which characterized so many in the revivalist and pietist traditions.[25]

To Disciples ignorance was a primary form of evil from which persons needed to be liberated. Wherever people did not know the truth of God, the liberating word must be proclaimed; communities without a Christian Church (Disciples variety) were known as "destitute places." The major task of the evangelist, as they conceived it, was to make the truth of God known and thus to deliver the ignorant. The pastor was a teacher, opening and explaining the Scripture. Any proper education, even in public school, would include a study of the Bible; in such a situation Campbell considered the teacher even more influential than the preacher. And he declared that "A week's debating is worth a year's preaching."[26]

The light of truth would scatter all darkness, not only of ignorance but of superstition. Uncharacteristically, they rarely stopped to define it, but presumably superstition meant any belief in supernatural power other than that specifically taught in Scripture. They cultivated skepticism toward contemporary Christian claims of miraculous or charismatic powers, relying rather on "positive" or objective assurance of the Spirit's presence. They knew, for example that they had the gift of the Holy Spirit because the New Testament promised it to those who had been baptized. They put no stock in any other "sign" or internal assurance.[27]

With the growth of the missionary movement, they saw the power of Christ emancipating the heathen races from the superstitions of paganism, whether animism or "high religion." Accepting as he did, on biblical "evidence" the reality of demons, Campbell held that their power is wholly destroyed "where the gospel has found its way." He told a Nashville audience that "Some arrogate to human science what has been the prerogative of the gospel alone." A dramatic story of liberation from the dark powers was told by the late Everard R. Moon, pioneer missionary to Congo (now Zaire). A Congolese evangelist had baptized some converts in a village, and the old witch doctor in an effort to halt the defections from the ancestral faith hung an exceedingly potent fetish over the door of the preacher's own hut. Many of the villagers fell into terror, for the fetish was certain to result in death to the offender. The evangelist rose to the occasion. In full view of all the villagers he tore the fetish from the doorpost, ripped it apart, and vigorously chewed up the potent "medicine" with a smile of triumph. He did not fall over dead. So, proclaimed the Disciples, the gospel liberates from ignorance, superstitution, and fear.[28]

Redemption from Sin and Death

Despite their conviction that one who heard the gospel might believe and repent without a special miracle of grace, the early Disciples stood with the classical Protestant Reformers in viewing humanity as lost in sin and needing redemption in Christ. In this respect, Campbell was closer to traditional Christian thought than most subsequent Disciples have been. In Adam's sin human nature fell from its natural state of virtue to a condition of rebellion and death. He speaks solemnly of the human situation:

Man is still great in his ruins. Once the most exact and beautiful similitude of the Great Original of universal being, he is still to be reverenced; and, when renewed in the moral image of his Maker, he is to be loved and admired not only as the noblest work of almighty power, but as the special and exclusive object of redeeming grace and mercy.[29]

The redemption which Disciples preached they saw operating in full response to human need. It frees from the guilt of sin, the power of sin, and the state of sin. In offering deliverance from guilt, it releases the Christian from the burden of a troubled conscience, putting to an end alienation from God and neighbor. In emancipating from the power of sin, it overcomes the love of evil and breaks the hold of negative habits. In delivering from the state of sin, it formally justifies the believer and bestows all the rights pertaining to a child of God. Disciples often used such language in juridical fashion, tending to lay most of their emphasis on baptism as a transaction which formally altered the sinner's state. So Frank Hamilton Marshall used to say that Disciples had not preached repentance with sufficient fervor, meaning that many had placed more stress on the formal efficacy of immersion than on pleading for a change of affections. But E. V. Zollars spoke of genuine change in terms of liberty:

There are two ways to govern men: One is by outward restriction, and one is by inward principle. . . . Before . . . true liberty is reached, inward principle must become the governing power. The law must be written on the heart. As long as law is external, man is a slave.[30]

Disciples could preach from experience the power of the gospel to redeem from destructive habits. G. Edwin Osborn told of a man whose life had begun with great promise until he fell victim for twenty years to the power of drink.

Losing health, job after job, his home, finally driving from his house children and wife, he went lower and lower, until one Saturday midnight in desperation he called the minister, saying

58

he could go no further and that unless he had help he intended to end it all.

After going to his room, fearing he was too drunk to be responsible, I challenged him to demonstrate his sincerity by coming to me completely sober by the middle of next week.

That he did, begging to be helped, asking for instruction, offering any kind of humble evidence to prove his sincerity.

In a few weeks he was baptized; in a few months his family returned, he secured professional employment again; in a couple of years he was elected deacon, and then church treasurer; and through it all a gentle, sainted character.

Thus the gospel became a power of personal liberation. Freedom in Christ found expression in the discipline of the disciple.[31]

Disciples also proclaimed the redemptive gospel as liberating the Christian from the fear of death. Listen to E. L. Powell of Louisville preaching on "Easter Hopes."

I need not speak of this hope as energizing life and character. We have felt "the power of an endless life" in our thoughts, which "pierce the night like stars"; in our aspirations, which proclaim that we were made for another world than this; in our dissatisfaction with the perishable, which tells us we were not born to die. We have recognized the energy of this hope in its sustaining influence when "troubles gathered thick and thundered loud."

And at last when death has stood before us demanding the countersign, we have whispered "Hope," and passed in serenity the line which divides the seen from the unseen. It has brought strength to the reformer in his heroic enterprise. It has sustained the scholar in his proclamation of new and unwelcome truth. It has enabled the martyr to meet the lurid glare of the flame with the victorious smile of peaceful resignation. And it has strengthened the humble sufferer on the bed of death to pass from earth with a paean of victory on his lips.[32]

So the Christian gospel as proclaimed by the evangelists and preachers brought liberty in its full existential character to those who believed the good news.

Liberation from Oppression

The task of liberating the human spirit cannot limit itself to the interior life. Even an existential analysis of human bondage throws a spotlight on the external shackles of social and economic oppression which hold down millions of persons in poverty, degradation, and hopelessness. In such a context of human exploitation, we must ask how the gospel addresses those who presumably benefit from the workings of an unjust system and those who obviously suffer from it. During recent years the theologies of liberation have engaged this question. While it seemed not too long ago that a deep rift had opened, separating Christians with an interior gospel from those who saw the word of God addressed to conditions of injustice, that gap appears to be closing. Both the World Conference of Evangelicals at Lausanne in 1974 and the Fifth Assembly of the World Council of Churches at Nairobi in 1975 affirmed a gospel which deals with the human condition in its totality. And Disciples have understood the freedom that is in Christ to involve release from oppressive social conditions as well as from inner enslavement.

The prominence of the millennium in the preaching of Campbell and Scott, as we saw in our first lecture, kept a hopeful vision of the amelioration of society before the eyes of Disciples. Yet their inability to perceive slavery as a religious issue muted the gospel to the oppressed. Furthermore, their understanding of the kingdom of God as synonymous with the church caused Disciples to see ecclesiological implications in the Scripture far more readily than demands upon society. Nevertheless, many of them participated in social movements for the expansion of liberty. They agitated for public schools. Their new colleges in the West were among the first in America to practice coeducation. (Two alumnae of Eureka College led in establishing the Christian Woman's Board of Missions.) Both women and men—the latter not unanimously!—spoke out for woman suffrage. Preachers, editors, and laypersons campaigned for prohibition, seeing it not as repressive legislation but as a means of freeing the people from drunkenness and poverty. A few Disciples participated in anti-war movements. Harold Gray suffered imprisonment as a conscientious objector during World War I. T. W. Phillips pressed for legislation to restrict the power of monopolies.

While Christian intellectuals in the East agitated for public righteousness under the name of the social gospel, Disciple editors in Cincinnati, St. Louis, and even Nashville also pressed for justice and compassion. In this century, Alva W. Taylor, James A. Crain, Walter W. Sikes, and Barton Hunter gave institutional leadership in social education and action. Samuel Guy Inman and Emory Ross engaged in labors on behalf of the oppressed in Latin America and Africa. R. H. Garfield Todd, a missionary of the churches in New Zealand, entered politics in Rhodesia and as prime minister undertook to achieve justice for the black majority; for his convictions he endured years of house arrest. Charles Clayton Morrison, Harold E. Fey, and Willard E. Shelton wielded vigorous editorial pens in the cause of freedom. Kirby Page stumped the country as a social evangelist and developed a theological rationale for pacifism based on the divine respect for human freedom.[33]

The preachers in the churches picked up the theme. In 1917 H. D. C. Machlachlan (our erstwhile cowboy) called for conversions that would transform individuals from selfishness and so regenerate society. Theology must be restated to make clear that God "hates social injustice." A new ideal of philanthropy— really not so new, for it was very like Alexander Campbell's— must replace old sentiments:

The new ideal would widen the scope of the word charity until it covered all disinterested efforts to better any sort of human condition, and at the same time seek to remove causes rather than alleviate effects. Social Service, again, is to be distinguished by its thorough-going democracy. It has robbed charity of its caste and condescension. It has stripped My Lady Bountiful of her silks and satins and bidden her live among the poor in social settlements. It has robbed My Lord Benevolent of his "grand air" and told him to be just in his business and clean in his political affiliations. Its ideals, in a word, are humanitarian just like those of the old philanthropy; but its methods are those of the ballot-box, the mass-meeting, the scientific investigation, the public playground, the Juvenile Court, the Civic Improvement League, etc.

Even a conservative evangelist, James Earl Ladd, wrote in 1934,

Your land shall shake and writhe when souls
You have oppressed shall flame in action!
When tortured mountains cry for justice.

J. Irwin Miller, industrialist and philanthropist, served as the first lay president of the National Council of Churches, and became a persuasive advocate in the business community for the extension of freedom:

Liberty for each of us is found not at all, unless it is found in a dominant sacrificial concern for the other fellow, and especially the deprived and disadvantaged. Property has no value for any of us unless each of us has a primary care for the property rights of the other fellow, and especially of the other fellow least able to look out for himself.[34]

A company of black Disciples gave significant early leader-

61

ship to the struggle of their people for dignity and equality. Preston Taylor led in organizing the National Convention; Merle Eppse publicized the cause in *The Christian Plea* and did the first significant work on the history of the black churches among Disciples. Cleo W. Blackburn pioneered in the field of community relations, preparing blacks for industrial jobs in the urban North and enabling them to acquire quality housing; he secured a congressional charter for the Board of Fundamental Education. Rosa Page Welch campaigned for the acceptance of her people and the integration of public accommodations. She sang her way around the world as one of the first blacks to travel Africa and Asia as a Christian ambassador of goodwill. Her odyssey under the auspices of the National Council of Churches prompted James H. Robinson to say,

One of the greatest things the American Churches have ever done was to send Rosa Page Welch around the world to sing to the people. Thousands have heard her. In Thailand the emperor used his influence to get the Roman Catholic church hall, the largest in the city, for her and she sang to a great audience.

In St. Louis, the late Norman Ellington addressed the urban crisis with a program of Change Through Involvement as an expression of his creed, "To be free in Christ is to be free to love across racial and economic lines."[35]

Something of Campbell's old millennial hope has persisted in the Disciple psyche. Not long before his death I heard Dean Frederick D. Kershner in his farewell address at the old School of Religion of Butler University (now Christian Theological Seminary). Looking back over nearly eight decades, he expressed his rejoicing for five developments during his lifetime:

(1) *I have lived in the nineteenth century (25 years), the greatest era of human culture, and the twentieth century (52 years), the century of revolution*
(2) *The Declaration of Human Rights of the United Nations— the greatest forward movement of the whole human race*
(3) *The birth of world community, the United Nations giving form to the hope of one world*
(4) *The release of atomic energy; the introduction of the Atomic Age may be the end for humanity or the beginning of a new Eden*
(5) *The birth of the ecumenical movement, giving promise for the realization of one church.*

The old classicist concluded with *Ave atque vale, moritari salutamus,* and a reference to Moses on Mount Pisgah looking across to the Promised Land which others were to enter.[36]

In contemporary America, younger Disciple theologians continue the commitment to freedom. Daniel Cobb has written provocative ethical analysis:

The real issue is whether or not the order which secures men's liberty is such that it also promotes human welfare; i.e., such that it provides real—as against theoretical—opportunity for individual and communal fulfillment.

William R. Barr addresses alienation and the struggle for liberation by going to the center of Christian theology:

In . . . the radical identification of God with the creature, enacted in the figure of Jesus, God has overcome the alienation of the creature and put this behind as an irretrievable past and set the creature on the way to a future which is life. It is this future (and life) that is "the freedom for which Christ has set us free" (Gal. 5). But this is a freedom exercised in love—the love that respects and seeks to empower the full humanity of the other. . . . Thus the life of freedom is a life lived in trust and responsibility to the liberating God who is its source, power, and goal.

. . . The God who is present in the ministry of Jesus is not a God whose presence (and power) is limited by, nor does it limit, creaturely freedom, but it is rather a God whose presence and power empowers the creature to a new and full human life in interrelation and interaction with others. The God who acts to liberate the creation in Christ is a God in relation to whom we are not free . . . in ourselves, but in whom we are free as we share in the ongoing history of God's empowering and liberating of others. Such a God is . . . a free and liberating God.

In a searching discussion of freedom and faithfulness, Clark M. Williamson relates freedom to community and to identification with "the liberating will of God." From the New Testament he notes "nine forms of slavery from which Jesus Christ liberates us." These are "disease, hunger, wealth, tyrants and oppressors, traditions, legalism, tribalism and racism, sin, and death." God's sufficient grace and the Christ who overcame death deliver us from all such forms of bondage to a life of joyful involvement.

Christian freedom means:
    to serve the needs and hurts of other people,
    to teach the Christian way,
    to live the Christian life of love,
    to contribute, generously, to the alleviation of suffering,
    to give aid with zeal,

> *to do acts of mercy with cheerfulness.*
> *Faith is being free!*

Thus in the language of Disciples most concerned to liberate humanity from oppressive social structures we discern the same gospel which the evangelists had addressed to the interior needs of the human heart—"Till the world was set right."[37]

Walking in Liberty

Did this gospel, we must ask, produce a sense of freedom in those who responded to it? Not in all, we must confess. Some impressive persons have left the Disciples, including Sidney Rigdon, Peter Burnett, Edwin Markham, John Muir, and Joseph Fort Newton. And some who remained with them had difficulty in laying hold on the liberty which is in Christ. But in almost any congregation we could gather up stories of saints who have studied the divine precepts and walked in freedom. Their Christian life was no somber affair. *I Would Do It Again,* declared F. E. Davison in the title of his book on the ministry. Amused by a young admirer's identification of the three "saints of the brotherhood"—Davy, G. Edwin Osborn, and Stephen J. England—he whimsically addressed the other two thereafter as St. Edwin and St. Stephen.[38]

At a more profound level, Hampton Adams once told a story about a memorable visit to Edwin Markham with a small group of Disciple ministers.[39] For two hours in the poet's book-lined house he read from his pieces. At length Dr. Adams observed that Markham had not read his familiar quatrain, "Outwitted." Their host fell silent for a time, then asked, "Would you care to hear the story back of those lines." He told of a great wrong once done by a partner who cheated Markham of a large sum of money. Hatred and the desire for vengeance seethed within him till they consumed his thoughts. He realized that he was no longer writing poetry. For months he was silent.

Remembering my old Campbellite mother, and how she used to insist on our forgiving others even when we felt we were in the right, I knew what I should have to do. I struggled with the matter, and at last decided that I must forgive my enemy. When I found I couldn't do that, I asked God to help me, and then wrote a letter to my former partner to that effect. Then strangely enough, while still at my desk, there came a flood of poetic inspiration, and whether it was my hand, or Another's, I wrote:

> He drew a circle and shut me out,
> Heretic, rebel, a thing to flout;
> But love and I had the wit to win,
> We drew a circle and took him in.

Or here is part of an evening prayer by Peter Ainslie, whose liberating ministry embraced personal, ecclesiastical, and social concerns:[40]

As Thou didst partake of our experience in sending Thy only begotten son among men, so we can only partake of Thy experience by living Thy life in Christ. Then show us the holiness of brotherly love and the beauty of sacrificing for each other's good; teach us how to forgive every wrong and to remember Thy own perfect grace and pardon; help us to hate a lie, a suspicion, and every unbrotherly thought and action; make us free men from the slavery of evil passion and every sinful habit; give to us purity of life, cleanness of heart, humility of spirit . . . by giving to us the consciousness that Thou art still our Father and we are brothers in Christ Jesus our Lord. Amen.

The passage just quoted indicates both a commitment to Christian freedom and a concurrent blindness to the oppressive sexism of traditional language, concerning which the women's liberation movement has begun to raise our consciousness. For more than a century Disciples have had a company of dedicated women serving effectively in posts of national leadership. But Disciples showed no particular discernment into the oppression of women and minorities by the customs of American society. Not till 1973 did they elect a woman to preside over their general assembly. This record contrasts with that of American Baptists who in 1977 chose their *sixth* woman president. Not till 1971 did Disciples name a black moderator. By the decade of the seventies Americans had begun to be sensitized in such matters, and Disciples took pride in demonstrating their new awareness, but they were not blazing new trails.[41]

Yet the commitment of Disciples to freedom was clear in intention if not always in perception. Typically the editor of *The Christian-Evangelist* wrote in 1924:

Nothing is impossible to a people who learn how to exercise their liberty in love and who chasten, clarify and temper their love by the wisdom which comes from above. Love, liberty, and truth— these are the things that build the church and conquer the world. Millions have died for liberty, more millions have died for love, and truth is the foundation of both.

In the work of evangelism Disciples saw themselves widening commitment to the truth which makes all people free.[42]

Education for Freedom

In their mission of liberating the human spirit Disciples placed reliance on two major instruments, evangelism and education. With respect to the latter, the founders enjoyed modest advantages. Thomas Campbell read theology under the tutelage of an older minister after completing the literary course at the University of Glasgow. Barton Stone attended a frontier academy, one of the "log colleges" of the back country. Alexander Campbell made use of the delay in his voyage to America occasioned by a shipwreck to study for a year in the University of Glasgow and in the Haldanean seminary as well; afterwards his father tutored him and he went on to give a remarkable demonstration of the possibilities of self-education. Walter Scott studied at the University of Edinburgh before coming to the New World. All four became teachers as well as preachers, and three were editors also.

They inhabited the same house of intellect as most educated persons of their time, for learning had not yet become highly specialized. They knew the liberal arts including a fair range of classical literature. They knew John Locke, the other major figures of the Enlightenment, and the Scottish philosophers of the Common Sense school. They knew some mathematics and pure science, especially geology and astronomy. They knew something of applied science—"I am a practical man," said the younger Campbell. They knew, above all else, the Bible. And Campbell was well versed in the church Fathers and in history.[43]

Intelligence and Liberty

Their theory of education conceived it as the culture or development of the student: it should be adapted to the human constitution. Accordingly, "man and woman should be educated in their entire personality" and also "in reference to the special *calling,* or the special *mission,* of each individual." In traditional fashion, they spoke of the liberal arts as liberating the mind of the student, though not, so far as I know, as liberating the works of culture which were studied. They came closer to another traditional way of talking about the humane letters—as studies which more fully humanize the student. So Campbell observed,

All that lies between barbarism and the highest civilization, all that distinguishes the rude American Indian and the most polished citizen, the barbarian and the Christian, has been

achieved by the learning, the science, the arts, the religion and the morals which colleges have nourished, cherished and imparted to the world.

In their thinking, a major element in education was moral culture, and this required the "Book of God." Campbell insisted that "a school, an academy, a college, without the Bible in it, is like a universe without a centre and without a sun."

Without it, you may create a popular gentleman, or a fashionable philosopher, at the meridian of London, Paris or Washington. But without it you cannot create a man, in all the nobility, moral grandeur and sublimity of his origin, relations and destiny in God's universe. A college or a school, therefore, adapted to the genius of human nature—to man as he is, and as he must be hereafter—cannot be found in Christendom, in the absence of a moral education founded upon the Bible, and the Bible alone, without the admixture of human speculations, or of science falsely so called.[44]

Although Campbell occasionally made a remark reminiscent of Tertullian in disparaging the literature of classical antiquity, with its "gods and goddesses—their amours and intrigues, their lusts and passions, their broils and battles," he accepted the essential value system of the humane studies. Hence he referred to Jesus as "the greatest philosopher that ever lived," the Great Teacher, the Supreme Philanthropist, the Great Lawgiver. He averred that "God himself, by plenary inspiration, educated the Bible philosophers, orators and scribes." Whatever belittling comments he might make about theology, he played the role of the intellectual to the hilt, whether as linguist, historian, philosopher, or orator. He followed developments in science, regarding all its discoveries as favorable to Christianity.[45] "The voice of nature will never contradict the voice of revelation. Nature and the Bible are both witnesses for God." He looked upon the entire universe, with all its ranks and orders, as marvelously interconnected—

and then all as related to the Supreme Intelligence, the fountain and source of all that is wise, and great, and good, and beautiful and lovely—the Parent of all being and of all joy; . . . nature's uncreated and unoriginated Author.

Campbell's thinking and work in education have received authoritative treatment elsewhere, most recently in President Perry E. Gresham's series of Reed Lectures.[46]

The academic tradition among Disciples continued the emphasis on the harmony between Christianity and the best in learning. They perceived this concord as resulting not merely from the coherence of all truth, which Campbell had observed, but also from the Christian impact on culture. So E. V. Zollars affirmed, early in this century,

The best in literature, the best in ethics, the best in government, the best in art, the best in music are the results of Christian influence and sentiment.

Even Disciples with conservative attitudes toward "worldly amusements" saw value in the masterpieces of literature. Johnson Bible College, for example, had strict rules against dancing, going to the theater, and other such perils. Once in Malcolm Norment's student days he slipped away from campus in order to see a traveling company's production of "Hamlet" or "Macbeth." It was a long, nervous walk back to the school, and—horror of horrors!—on a lonely stretch of road he met President Ashley S. Johnson driving his buggy into town. Dr. Johnson must have surmised where the youth had been. He spoke to him courteously and went on his way. Contrary to all accustomed procedure, he never did inquire about the young man's absence.[47]

The function of the church college was to provide society with leaders furnished with a complete culture, intellectual, moral, and religious. "The richest mine in any community is its mind," Campbell told an audience in Appalachia. *"Educated mind must govern, and does govern, the world, and the universe of which it is a constituent part."* He laid upon the class of 1847 at Bethany College "the claims which your country, the church of God, and the human race have upon you." And E. V. Zollars hymned the liberating effect of Christian education:

If the young of this generation are made what they ought to be, in the next generation the social life will be pure and refined, the intellectual life will be bright and elevated, the political life will be honest and patriotic, and the religious life will be zealous and intelligent.

"All education," in the thinking of Edward Scribner Ames, might be said "to be in a true sense an extension of freedom."[48]

Educators among Disciples, committed to the principle of political equality, long spoke of an "aristocracy of merit." It consisted of persons to be honored for learning and character and motivated by the conviction, *noblesse oblige.* To another graduating class at Bethany, Campbell made the point:

But especially are you under obligation to advocate just views of education, and to plead for its universal diffusion throughout society. You are to consider yourselves as charged with this duty

*from the special call given you in this dispensation of Divine
Providence. You enter the drama of life under peculiar advantages—Americans by birth, citizens of the United States, the
gifted sons of a gifted ancestry, a majority of you Christians, and
all of you ought to be. You have yourselves laboriously passed
through the whole course of a liberal education. You have read
Grecian and Roman history, philosophy, poetry, and eloquence,
in the language of Greece and Rome. You have made the grand
tour of the sciences, physical, intellectual and moral. You are
well read in mathematics, pure and mixed, and in the mysteries
of number and magnitude. Few of your juvenile contemporaries
will enter the arena of public life with more advantages than you
possess.*

Clearly, the function of a liberal education was to liberate
both the students and the larger society in which they would
take their place. The increase of education could effect a "great
moral revolution" and enlarge the area of liberty without
resort to war. In Campbell's words, *"Intelligence and freedom
are but two names for the same thing."*[49]

Academies and Teachers

The establishment of schools became a major occupation of
Disciples. Later on the scene and smaller in numbers than
Congregationalists, Presbyterians, Baptists, or Methodists,
they founded fewer continuing colleges than did these others.
Nevertheless Claude E. Spencer's list of schools begun by the
Disciples contains 485 entries, most of which did not survive.
About thirty liberal arts institutions maintain ties with the
various strands of the movement today.[50]

Along with other Protestants, nineteenth century Disciples
propagandized for universal education in public schools as essential to a free society. Campbell stood in the forefront: *"the
great end of all government is to teach men to govern themselves."* Garfield declared that without popular education
"neither freedom nor justice can be permanently maintained."[51] Early in the twentieth century, Vachel Lindsay was
moved to ask:

> *Who can pass a district school
> Without the hope that there may wait
> Some baby-heart the books shall flame
> With zeal to make his playmates great. . . !*

And despite the preference of many in the early days for
overtly Christian institutions, Disciples have taken their part
in the development of the public universities. They furnished

presidents of the University of Missouri and the University of Oregon in their formative years, and others have held high posts in such institutions down to the present moment. Before the tax-supported schools introduced the study of religion, the Christian Woman's Board of Missions established Bible chairs at the universities of Michigan, Kansas, Texas, and Virginia. Disciples also gave leadership to a similar venture on an ecumenical scale, the Bible College of Missouri, set up "to teach the Bible in the university atmosphere."[52]

With respect to the education of the ministry, new emergents in the world of thought and the life of the churches brought two divergent developments among the Disciples in the twentieth century. On the one hand, they established graduate seminaries, as well as houses or foundations affiliated with major divinity schools. In protest against the "liberal" position of these schools (and of the liberal arts institutions as well), more conservative Disciples launched a large number of Bible colleges offering an undergraduate course designed to prepare students to preach. To a greater or lesser degree these schools rejected the liberal arts curriculum, concentrating on the content of Scripture, "doctrine," and skills of ministry. In general, the schism between the Christian Church (Disciples of Christ) and the undenominational fellowship of Christian Churches and Churches of Christ followed lines drawn by these divergent patterns of ministerial education. Time does not permit the tracing out of this division, with its obvious social and cultural basis, nor developing the implications of the alternative types of ministerial education for the liberation of the human spirit.[53]

It would be a mistake, however, to think of the academic enterprise primarily in terms of institutions. For Disciples in every generation have recognized the supreme importance of the teacher in the process of education. In the days when their schools were small, self-contained communities in which the students lived for four years in intimate and daily contact with a miniscule faculty, the role of the teacher was decisive, not only as instructor and disciplinarian, but also as model and friend. To read the memoirs of the nineteenth century is to come across repeated confessions of personal indebtedness to one professor or another. Garfield's aphorism about Mark Hopkins of Williams College—a great teacher outside the Disciple orbit—has been often heard, though usually misquoted. The one essential in education was "a true teacher."

Give me a log hut, with only a simple bench, Mark Hopkins on one end, and I on the other, and you may have all the buildings, apparatus, and libraries without him.

70

Disciples should also know Garfield's touching tribute to Almeda A. Booth of Hiram.[54]

Generation after generation the teachers made their contribution. One day in 1939 Dean Frank Hamilton Marshall preached in chapel at Phillips University on "The Ninth Commandment." In a sermon of eloquence and power, he quoted without notes from Scripture, the Vedas, Pindar, Plato, Shakespeare, Ruskin, and many others. Coming out of chapel. Dean Arty Boyd Smith remarked to a student, "I've just been thinking of the difference between a redwood and a mesquite."[55]

Almost immediately after the death of James A. Garfield, his longtime friend B. A. Hinsdale set to work on a "Hiram College Memorial," a book which he entitled *President Garfield and Education.* It included sketches of the school's history and of Garfield's activities there, as well as a dozen speeches which he had made in public life on the subject of education. It also contained a number of addresses given at the special Hiram College memorial service held in Cleveland while the body of the slain president lay in state. The honesty of Hinsdale's own word on that occasion reaches across the years, revealing both the greatness of a spirit enriched by a Christian education and the mysteries before which even such a spirit must bow.

He has left us his life and his spirit. Storm and war and strife are all over . . . .

Let me ask, why was all this permitted? Why was the assassin allowed to strike him down? Why were not the prayers of the people granted? Why did the night-raven never lift his wings, and fly away? Why was the Most High deaf? And why did the heavens give no sign? What a strange providence! How can it fit into any plan of divine wisdom and love? Thus far I have scarcely tried to answer these questions, though they have pressed upon me many an hour. It is a great test of faith in God. But Garfield believed in God. He thought that an increasing purpose runs through the ages, and comprehends the lives of men; and I think so too. Still, hitherto I have been able to do little more than say, "Lord, I believe: help thou mine unbelief!" For myself, I must leave the problem to the future. History will no doubt discover and disclose what passes my power to comprehend.[56]

The Congregation as the School of Christ

As close as the colleges were to the church, especially in the first century of the movement, the church itself remained the major instrument and arena of education. The Great Teacher

71

was, of course, Jesus Christ, and he had commissioned his disciples not only to evangelize but to teach. Listen once again to Hinsdale:

Christianity consists of a Gospel and a discipline. Out of this fundamental distinction arise the two distinctive functions of the Christian ministry. One is to preach this Gospel, the other to teach this discipline: preaching and teaching.[57]

These two tasks devolved, in Campbell's doctrine of ministry, on two of its "standing and immutable" orders, evangelists and bishops, while deacons carried responsibility for service. The evangelists were itinerant preachers and founders of churches; in the first two generations they constituted what we would call the educated or professional ministry. The bishops Disciples today know as elders; in the nineteenth century they were commonly called pastors and teachers. Eldership was the chief local office of ministry, collegial because of the doctrinal insistence on a plurality of elders, and unsalaried. The chief difference between then and now is that these local bishops were not perceived as representatives of the laity sharing responsibilities with the ministry; in the eyes of an early congregation of Disciples, the elders were the ministers. They presided at the table of the Lord and they provided the teaching or sermon, except on the infrequent occasions when a visiting preacher (evangelist) was present. Their task was the edification, or building up of the church; their teaching a simple commentary on a passage of scripture or an exposition of doctrine. This system of ministry readily cared for the needs of pioneer communities, but Campbell advanced it as the biblically authorized order of the church. If it freed the early congregations from dependence on a professional clergy (a class not particularly popular on the frontier), it also put teaching at the heart of congregational life. The emphasis on "head religion" prevailed, and elders who knew the Bible well and read one of the Disciple journals with care taught the doctrine with a great concern for faithfulness. From the beginning, the rationale for establishing Disciple colleges was not just to educate preachers but to provide persons in the various professions equipped to serve as elders.[58]

The emphasis on teaching in the congregation was consistent with the Disciples' love of liberty. It comported with their understanding of Jesus, concerning whom Hinsdale wrote,

He wholly excludes from His system the element of external force. He never resorts to material means, to physical pains and penalties. His kingdom is a kingdom of the mind, His reign a reign of the spirit.

72

Alexander Procter of Independence, Missouri, discussed the process:[59]

Jesus said . . . . "Go and teach." That is the means, the power, that is going to create the work of change in the human mind . . . . This is what the apostle means when he says, "Put off the old man that is corrupt according to the deceitful lusts." The "old man" was the ignorant man, the man of insensibility, the man who was going wrong, and "put on the new man"; and he is made new by knowledge—that is the first thing, the usual process. He is made new in righteousness . . . . he takes hold of the beautiful truth and the goodness of God as illustrated in Christ.

Besides the "speaking" of the elders in the Sunday services, Disciples developed other important procedures for teaching. The preaching of the evangelists turned a protracted meeting into a course of lessons on the basic elements of the faith; they often diagrammed their sermons on charts or blackboards as they preached. The weekly prayer meeting normally included a period of Bible study, and the Sunday school early became an important instrument of teaching. Campbell himself had said of Robert Raikes, that

though of no remarkable genius, by setting on foot the Sunday-school system, [he] has done for the world more than all the conquerors of nations, founders of empires and great political demagogues whose names are inscribed upon the rolls of fame.

With the founding of the Christian Woman's Board of Missions, auxiliary programs were soon developed for children and young people. The Women's Christian Temperance Union held similar sessions for them. The Young People's Society of Christian Endeavor, by the turn of the century, became a standard fixture in vital congregations. Today when elaborate programs of public education, television, and opportunities for travel provide the younger generation with such breadth of experience, we tend to overlook the contribution which the activities of the congregation made to expanding the horizons in an earlier time when cultural opportunities were meager. Here is a word from "Mother" Ross, written just over a half-century ago:

A teacher in Indiana told me she could always tell the boys and girls of earnest missionary mothers. They have a clear conception of the far-off countries, the habits and customs of strange people and the world's great need, by hearing these questions discussed in their own homes.

And, we may add, in their churches.[60]

In his millennial poem on "The Illinois Village," from which we have already quoted the lines about the district school, Vachel Lindsay celebrated the church also:

> Who can pass a village church
> By night in these clean prairie lands
> Without a touch of Spirit-power?
> So white and fixed and cool it stands—
> . . . .
>
> The trees that watch at dusty noon
> Breaking its sharpest lines, veil not
> The whiteness it reflects from God,
> Flashing like Spring on many an eye,
> Making clean flesh that once was clod.

The new generation of fulltime pastors, or professional ministers, who assumed the leadership of the congregations toward the end of the nineteenth century contributed in a large way to the education of the church. In the new era of urban culture they assisted the Disciples in emancipating themselves from the simpler, but sometimes rigidly held, formulations of an earlier time. Often they worked in the face of complaints that they were straying from the old paths, and earnest, if respectful, struggles occurred between an elder who saw his vocation as a "hound of the Lord" and a minister with a broader view of truth. One such preacher, who used his pulpit to educate not only a congregation but his part of the country in the 1890s, was Alexander Procter of Independence, Missouri. He considered it his responsibility to inform his hearers of the new developments in scientific thought and their implications for Christian faith.

I am looking at the fact, and I tell you that no educated man believes any more that this universe was created instantaneously, as we see it now, or in a few thousand years. What is called the nebular hypothesis is almost as universally accepted as the knowledge of the law of gravitation.

Yet the contemplation of "these forces . . . at work" left the preacher with the conviction that "there was a plan" for earth in the mind of the Author: "it was meant to be the home of man." Proctor rejoiced in the discoveries of the scientists:

The advance of mankind . . . has been made by the efforts of the intellect in making these discoveries. God has his witnesses everywhere. Sir Isaac Newton was a witness, sent to bear testimony to the great question of gravitation; Herschel in his time was a witness for the movement of the stars; Galileo, the first who was willing to suffer for it; Hugh Miller and Lyell were

74

witnesses, adequate to testify to the truths of geology; and so in all the departments of science.

Elsewhere he expounded the thinking of Agassiz and Darwin. And all this in 1892, not in Brooklyn or Boston, but at the "jumping-off place" in western Missouri almost half a century after his years as a student at Bethany College![61]

In Chicago, Edward Scribner Ames, minister of Hyde Park (later University) Church of Disciples and also professor of philosophy in the university, used to publish in the weekly calendar a formulation of the ideals held before that congregation:

This church practices union; has no creed; seeks to make religion as intelligent as science; as appealing as art; as vital as the day's work; as intimate as the home; as inspiring as love.

Thoughtful Disciples attracted to liberal religion rejoiced in the openness of their heritage. The historic emphasis on freedom of opinion seemed to them to give Disciples particular appeal in the new intellectual climate of the twentieth century.[62]

Twenty-five years ago I heard Edgar DeWitt Jones present his celebrated lecture on "Pulpit Princes of the Disciples." Like the title, most of the preachers he discussed belonged to the early part of this century. The list included Z. T. Sweeney, E. L. Powell, George Hamilton Combs, Burris Jenkins, Peter Ainslie, A. W. Fortune, R. H. Miller, Roger T. Nooe, Frederick W. Burnham, P. H. Welshimer, and others. With few exceptions, these preachers were regarded as liberals. The preponderance may prompt the question whether or not there is a connection between an open theology and greatness in the pulpit. But one thing is clear. These men gave themselves to the struggle with new ideas and to helping their people come to terms with the issues. They were teachers of the church in no trivial sense. They were willing to battle for the truth as they saw it. [63]

During the turbulent 1960s Albert M. Pennybacker and I were talking with a group of seminarians about the ministry and the church. One of the students, protesting the conservatism he perceived in congregational circles, asked indignantly, "But will the people permit the freedom of the pulpit?" Dr. Pennybacker gave a clear answer: "The only way you will get your freedom is to take it." To a gratifying extent, when ministers have used their liberty responsibly in fulfilling their duty to teach, the churches have sustained them. Even when the churches have not, those ministers have still been free.

75

The Education of the Church

In the decision of 1849 to conduct the convention as a mass meeting and to carry on missions through a society of individuals, Alexander Campbell lost the battle for a general "church organization." It took Disciples a long time after that to discover the church beyond the congregation. Not till 1968 were they ready to speak of the Christian Church (Disciples of Christ) as an ecclesiastical body. But the reality was present in their experience long before their ecclesiology would permit them to verbalize it. From the beginning the life of the "brotherhood" at large also served as a school of Christ.

A diverse company of editors carried on a vigorous educational ministry among their readers. As early as the year 1831-32, for example, in Jacksonville, Illinois alone, 22 subscribers received Stone's *Christian Messenger* and 15 Campbell's *Millennial Harbinger*. The journals of the movement stimulated the cause of "free discussion." For years *The Christian-Evangelist* carried J. H. Garrison's ditty expressing his editorial commitments. It began,

> *For the Christ of Galilee,*
> *For the truth which makes men free. . . .*[64]

The missionary enterprise enlarged the vision of the churches. Archibald McLean's *Circuit of the Globe* to visit the foreign fields in 1895 was a brotherhood event which aroused great excitement. (How many Disciples had previously circumnavigated the earth?) As the Sunday school movement matured into the religious education movement, great impetus was given to personal growth and expanding freedom. In pioneering the young people's conferences, for example, Cynthia Pearl Maus and Adeline Goddard opened new worlds to a generation of youth.[65]

A major step in the education of the church was the work of the colleges and seminaries in securing the principle of academic freedom in church-related institutions. The supportive response to the College of the Bible in the decision of its board in 1917 to stand by Professors Bower, Fortune, and Snoddy preserved the integrity of intellectual life among the Disciples—and contributed to the development of another schism.[66]

Meanwhile the activity of the Campbell Institute gave encouragement to liberty in intellectual inquiry. Founded in 1896 by a small group of Disciples who were university graduates, the Institute took as its emblem a cross formed by the Greek words ALETHEIA and ELEUTHERIA, truth and freedom. It is difficult to convey to a contemporary audience the mingled

sense of elation and daring which forty years ago swept over a
student brave enough to attend the sessions of the Institute in
the late hours after the program of an International Convention had closed. The fact that the open discussion of theological
ideas could cause so much excitement, and even the imputation
of guilt, indicates that all Disciples had not yet fully achieved
intellectual freedom. But the fact that issues of a type once
considered explosive are now openly discussed not only in the
colleges and seminaries, but on the floor of the General Assembly suggests that a new level of freedom has been attained.
Recognizing this fact, the Campbell Institute voted to dissolve
and adjourned *sine die* in 1975.[67]

I mention one further development in the education of the
church. After a century of organized life, Disciples had nearly
reached a point of readiness for a new departure in their self-
understanding and institutional relationships. But they were
still confused by their perception of their own past. They felt an
obligation of loyalty to a set of concepts which, they hesitated
to admit, no longer squared with their conscientious practice or
their best instincts regarding the church. Believing that only
intensive, honest thought could free the brotherhood for its own
future, the Board of Higher Education and the United Christian Missionary Society in 1956 jointly authorized the appointment of a Panel of Scholars. The remit was to "re-
examine" the "beliefs and doctrines" of the Disciples "in a
scholarly way." In the words of its chairman, W. B. Blakemore,

*The Panel was not asked to do the brotherhood's thinking for
it and to come up with the answers. It was asked to discover for
our people the issues worth talking about so that there might be
amongst us less talking in circles and more talking to the point.
The Panel was never commissioned to write a new theology for
our churches. What it did contract to do was to search out and
clarify the theological, biblical, sociological, and historical issues involved in our practical life. The identification of truly
relevant issues would enable our agency leaders and our pastors
to ignore obsolete matters and save untold man hours in the
extensive discussions necessary to properly reasoned discussions
in a body which values democratic procedures. With a due sense
of responsibility the Panel accepted this task.[68]*

Meeting twice a year for five and a half years, the Panel
produced, considered, and circulated for use by more than sixty
discussion groups throughout the country an impressive number of papers. These were published in 1963 in three volumes
under the title, *The Renewal of Church: The Panel Reports.*
They represented a dialogue with their past which enabled

Disciples to free themselves from that past and to engage in a fresh way the issues involved in "brotherhood restructure." Those issues were theological fully as much as practical. By the time the Panel concluded its labors, the Commission on Restructure was already at work. And in 1968, the Kansas City Assembly adopted *A Provisional Design for the Christian Church* (Disciples of Christ). In the school of Christ which is the church Disciples had found freedom of spirit to adopt a larger ecclesiology and a more responsible mode of working in their institutional life. They could now speak of the church in its congregational, regional, and general manifestations. They could take corporate decisions as a church while continuing to prize for members and congregations the freedom and integrity they had so long maintained.

"The Glorious Liberty of the Children of God"

We began this lecture by speaking of existential dimensions of freedom. We have explored some aspects of the history of Disciples as they contributed to the liberation of the human spirit. We have noted the liberty which Disciples have sought to advance through evangelism and education. Their witness has made for a realization of freedom in the lives of many persons and in the common life of the church itself.

I do not wish to romanticize the story. For even though Disciples have talked much of liberty from the beginning, they have had their own set of difficulties in receiving and practicing it. Their history shows some hard examples of lovelessness and rigidity and legalism. Nor does everything that passes for liberation turn out to be such. Right now our society is going through a time of much questioning and of repudiating many long accepted standards in the name of personal freedom. It is not at all clear to me that persons who have thrown off all the traditional relationships and restraints are either happy or free. What I mean by the liberation of the spirit is not that total renunciation of obligation to anyone but myself which is so much in the air today. Rather I mean to commend freedom in Christ. I mean what Paul Tillich termed theonomy in distinction from heteronomy or autonomy. I mean what St. Augustine commended when he said, "Love God and do as you please." What one pleases who loves God, of course, is to love one's neighbor and to grow in the likeness of God.

I would conclude in a quite personal way, not with any further theorizing but by example. Commonly when we deal with the history of a religious movement, we devote most of our attention to the founders. In contrast with that approach, I have attempted in these lectures to take some note of the broader sweep of the history of Disciples as a liberty-loving people. Even so, we have a great tendency to forget that our history includes all our yesterdays, including just yesterday and the hours that have already passed today. I want to suggest, therefore, what I mean by the liberation of the human spirit by calling to mind three Disciples who were only recently taken by death. To me they exemplify freedom understood as positive emancipation, as realization of inherent possibility. I speak of Walter W. Sikes, George G. Beazley, Jr., and William Barnett Blakemore, Jr.

Walter Sikes (1896-1966) grew up among the Churches of Christ in Texas. From Abilene Christian College he came to Vanderbilt Divinity School and then went on to Union Theological Seminary. As his thinking flowed in broader channels, he found greater congeniality of mind among the "progressive" Disciples and identified with that wing of the movement. For some years he taught at Berea College. Then he carried responsibility for social education and social action with the United Christian Missionary Society. In 1952 he came to the faculty of Christian Theological Seminary, where we were colleagues. In retirement he taught at Vanderbilt and at Eureka College. As the moving spirit in the founding of the Association of Disciples for Theological Discussion he left an important legacy. In his efforts to trace out the root of the problems which had perplexed him in his own pilgrimage, he made an intensive study of the history of Disciples and produced a massive manuscript, too large for publication, which brought to bear his competence in biblical, historical, psychological, sociological, and theological disciplines. That manuscript is now in the archives of the Disciples of Christ Historical Society. He published many articles searching in their insight, a book on Søren Kierkegaard, and other studies. He was a superb teacher. More than that, he was a gracious friend and an engaging conversationalist. One could talk with him for hours on any subject—the disciplines I have mentioned, the issues before the brotherhood, ecumenics, politics, world affairs, literature, music, art, baseball, fishing, or just "life"—and be instructed from the depth of his erudition and insight. He incarnated the liberation of the human spirit.[69]

George Beazley (1914-1973) was a Kentuckian, a graduate of Centre College and College of Bible. As a pastor in Missouri and Oklahoma he drew to his churches the inquiring minds of his community. He read with unbelievable range and insight in literature and the arts and he kept up with the scholarly study of the New Testament as if he had been a professor in a graduate school. When he came to head the Council on Christian Unity he brought a joy in dialogue, a love for Disciple tradition, and a commitment to the goal of a united church which soon had a large part of the brotherhood sharing his enthusiasm. He made his *News on Christian Unity,* familiarly called "Beazley Buzz," the most avidly read ecumenical publication in the world because of his fascinating personal reflections on the developing dialogue. He founded *Mid-Stream* as a journal of ecumenical discussion and through its pages made a large contribution to the maturing theological enterprise among Disciples. He edited a history of the brotherhood, the title of which tells much about his mind: *The Christian Church (Disciples of Christ): An Interpretative Examination in the Cultural Context.* He loved life—that meant good food in a distinguished atmosphere, travel in every part of the world, the traditions of Kentucky, the theater, concerts, art galleries, ideas, and books, books, books. Unlike any other office I have ever seen in a denominational headquarters, his was lined with books on every wall, its desks and tables piled so high with books that one could scarcely find room for a conference. He read them, and he shared the ideas in them. He wore out his Greek New Testament. He loved the brotherhood. He loved the church ecumenical. He loved the United States of America and its democratic traditions. The violence and irrationality of the 1960s deeply distressed him. In 1973 he traveled to Moscow on an ocumenical mission, and there with a suddenness that stunned us all he died. The last piece he filed for Beazley Buzz told of visiting historic cathedrals, of wondering how or when Christianity in Russia would again have full liberty to reassert itself with power in the culture, and of praying there for the coming of that freedom.[70]

Barnett Blakemore (1912-1975) was born the son of a minister in Australia and came to this country in his youth. A graduate of Washington University and of the University of Chicago (from which he received A.M., D.B., and Ph.D. degrees), he became dean of the Disciples Divinity House there in 1945 and served until his death thirty years later. During all that time he rendered to the Disciples a ministry of theological labor, marked with concern for the practical life of the church, as though he had been the canon of a cathedral. Before I had ever met him, his bride-to-be characterized him as a broad-

80

ocean, deep-river, high-mountain type of man, and he was that, with remarkable amplitude of mind, an impressive range of learning, and unremitting devotion to the church. He served on boards and commissions past counting, chaired the Panel of Scholars, worked at the center of the process of brotherhood restructure, attended the Second Vatican Council as an observer, and was elected president of the World Convention of Churches of Christ. He published articles of great penetration as well as several books, including *The Cornerstone and the Builders,* a suggestive essay in pastoral theology; *The Discovery of the Church: A History of Disciple Ecclesiology,* his Reed Lectures; and *Quest for Intelligence in Ministry.* He was an inspiring liturgist and a preacher of great intellectual and spiritual power. In any subject, as lecturer, author, or conversationalist, his ideas scintillated, and they were relevant. He too delighted in the world of art and literature. A minor masterpiece was his 1963 address to the Disciples of Christ Historical Society, which took note that we then stood about 200 years from Thomas Campbell, about 400 years from William Shakespeare. He entitled it, "If Tom is Half as Old as Will. . . ?" and presented insightful correlations between the thought of the elder Campbell and the bard of Avon.[71]

In the death of these three men, Disciples have lost great spirits from their midst. I confess to many pangs of loneliness as I have longed for the opportunity to talk once again with them about present concerns, to renew with them the deep commitments which we shared, to feel the strong support of their minds and hearts. I have not yet found anyone else like them, at once so civilized in intellect, so faithful to the gospel, so free at heart. But the sense of loss measures the magnitude of their contributions to the church at large and especially to Disciples of Christ in our own time. When we think of them we know what is meant by the liberation of the human spirit in the glorious liberty of the children of God.

3. Freedom for a United Church

The Integrity of the People of God

Stand fast in the freedom with which Christ has freed us

—*Galatians 5: 1*

Christian people are now confronted by a momentous question: *Will the church of Jesus Christ be free for its own future?* That query bears directly on the church's integrity in two important senses: (1) its liberty to be its authentic self, the true people of God and (2) its liberty to realize its own unity. Is it free to find its integrity as one holy catholic and apostolic church in the late twentieth century?

This is no idle question. Twenty years ago ecumenists like W. F. Garrison were pressing the query: Can the church have both freedom and unity?[1] That issue still presses. But we must put it another way: Can the church really be the church without being free and united? Can it be authentically Christian if it seeks its freedom in divisiveness? These questions call us back to our dependence on the Spirit, to the truth in the old Shaker hymn,

> *'Tis the gift to be simple,*
> *'Tis the gift to be free.*

Many churches have professed the love of freedom. One of the prices we pay for our separation from one another as Christians is our ignorance that others also prize the values we cherish in our little version of the true faith. In the early years of my ecumenical involvement, the late Dr. Douglas Horton once invited me to his office as general minister of the old Congregational-Christian Churches (before the union with the Evan-

82

gelical and Reformed Church to form the United Church of Christ). There on the mantle I read the inscription: Faith, Freedom, Fellowship. It was the motto of his denomination. Again and again in ecumenical discussions I have recognized the allegiance to liberty, sometimes in unexpected quarters. It comes out often in the fear that church union is an evil plot to take our freedom away from us.

The church's concern with its own liberty and integrity has great secular relevance. When he debated Robert Owen on revealed religion and Bishop Purcell on the Protestant principle, Alexander Campbell was engaging issues crucial for the character of American society. Recently an aging Spanish Communist, a life-long revolutionist, likened the new independence from Moscow on the part of Communist Parties in Western Europe to Martin Luther's rebellion against Rome. "We had our Pope, our Vatican," he said, but now "We must see that each individual has his private life. . . . [A] person's preferences of friends, of music and literature . . . has nothing to do with the party." The fascinating thing about these remarks is that a secularist arguing for freedom from a monolithic system finds his model within the history of church. Our present inquiry into the church's freedom could also have relevance for the life of the world.[2]

To continue, then, our reflections on the involvement of Disciples with issues of liberty, we address ourselves to three considerations:

1) *The movement as an effort to secure freedom in the church*
2) *The way in which this experiment in liberty has proved out*
3) *Resources from the experience of Disciples for the church of the future*

A word about method. In the two previous lectures I have operated primarily as a historian with some theological interest. In this lecture I shall be carrying on more of an inner dialog between two parts of myself, historian and amateur ecumenical theologian. And since I deal with current developments, the focus shifts toward that wing of the movement which I know best, the Christian Church (Disciples of Christ).

Experiment in Freedom

We begin with some reflections on the Disciples' efforts to secure liberty within the church. We have seen that theirs is a church formed in the atmosphere of freedom. Their commitment to liberty shaped their religion as well as their politics.

83

Freedom-Fighters on the Frontier

Those early American pioneers who took the name Christian for their churches rebelled against ecclesiastical practices which they felt to be tyrannical. Their varied careers as reformers began in an appeal for freedom. James O'Kelly resisted the new appointive powers assumed by Bishop Asbury and underscored the issue by calling his church *Republican* Methodist before settling on the simple title Christian. In New England, the Christian preachers Elias Smith and Abner Jones teamed up with Freewill Baptists to protest the doctrines of Calvinism. In the early West, Barton W. Stone and his Presbyterian collaborators withdrew from the Synod of Kentucky to assert their freedom to work with preachers of other denominations in the revivals. Stone also insisted on the right to hold theological views which he found consistent with the word of God, even though his straightlaced brethren deemed them heretical. Later he and his colleagues dissolved their Springfield Presbytery, willing to "sink into union with the body of Christ at large," in order to "taste the sweets of gospel liberty" simply as Christians.[3]

Thomas Campbell's trouble with Chartiers Presbytery began in 1807 with his exercise of freedom as a pastor in violation of ecclesiastical law. On the sparsely settled frontier where he found settlers deprived of ministry, he was accused of preaching within the bounds of another minister's parish, of advocating that ruling elders should "exhort publically in vacant congregations," and of failing to "fence the table" by insisting that all who came to communion subscribe to the fine points of the Westminster Confession. Rather than compromise his liberty as a minister, a liberty for which he believed he had biblical support, he incurred censure from his Synod and finally withdrew from its authority.[4]

Youthful rebellion seethed in the soul of Alexander Campbell that year he studied in Glasgow, building up pressure against the rigidity of the Anti-Burgher Seceder Church, heated by the witness of the Haldaneans to the simplicity of primitive Christianity. He executed his own declaration of ecclesiastical independence by turning in his communion token and walking away from a system of regulations he did not find in Scripture. For the next dozen years he played the iconoclast, inveighing against all the schemes and "traditions of men." As the number of Disciples grew under Scott's evangelism and as they emerged from sojourn with the Baptists, he gave himself more constructively to guiding the movement in an impressive career as editor, educator, debater, and orator. He asserted his liberation from his own earlier rigidity and negativism, professing never to have subscribed to the doctrine, "once in error always in error."[5]

If Walter Scott began his association with the Campbells less as a pilgrim of freedom than as a convert to the New Testament as sole rule, he nevertheless found it the means of liberating thousands both from the repressive dogma of election and from the revivalist pattern of conversion, which left hundreds of phlegmatic persons distressed by their sins but unblessed by any interior cataclysm as a sign from the Holy Spirit. His common-sense, biblical presentation of the positive "steps of salvation" became a gospel of liberation to many.

The dynamic which propelled the founders into leadership of this "American religious movement" was a quest for Christian liberty within the church.

A Continuing Disposition toward Freedom

If you have ever paused to read the inscription concerning Disciples of Christ in the Entrance Porch to the Thomas W. Phillips Memorial, you must have observed the way in which the love of liberty dominates the ethos of the people who there describe themselves. Their "pioneers," runs the inscription were persons "of the adventurous spirit of the new age of Freedom and Enlightenment."[6] They "held these truths to be self-evident":

> *THAT MEN ARE ENDOWED BY*
> *GOD WITH EQUAL RIGHTS TO THINK*
> *AND ACT FOR THEMSELVES IN ALL*
> *MATTERS OF RELIGIOUS BELIEF*
> *AND PRACTICE:*
> *THAT A DIVIDED CHURCH*
> *IS SIN AND THE SPIRIT OF LOVE AND*
> *UNITY, LIBERTY AND CONCORD, IS TO*
> *BE RESTORED BY CASTING OFF THE*
> *SHACKLES OF HUMAN TRADITIONS*
> *AND RETURNING TO THE ORIGINAL*
> *FAITH AND ORDER OF THE CHURCH*
> *OF CHRIST:*
> *THAT BELIEF IN JESUS THE*
> *CHRIST AND OBEDIENCE TO HIM AS*
> *LORD IS THE ONLY TEST OF CHRIS-*
> *TIAN CHARACTER AND THE ONLY*
> *BOND OF CHRISTIAN UNION.*

The motif of freedom—political, personal, churchly—runs

through the popular slogans in which Disciples sought to concentrate the essence of their movement, and which they repeated with fervor:

In essentials unity, in opinions liberty, in all things charity.

+ + +

Where the Scriptures speak, we speak; where the Scriptures are silent, we are silent.

+ + +

No creed but Christ, no book but the Bible, no law but love, no name but the divine.

+ + +

We are not the only Christians, but we are Christians only.

+ + +

The restoration of primitive Christianity, its doctrines, its ordinances, and its fruits.

If the last of these fails to mention Christian liberty specifically, it was perceived as setting forth the program for both liberty and unity, and it went without saying that one of the choicest "fruits" was the freedom of the Christian.

Their commitment to freedom has profoundly affected the way in which Disciples have perceived other religious bodies. The strain of anti-Catholicism which ran in their blood until the healing miracle of the Second Vatican Council owed more to their fear of Rome's authoritarianism than to their conviction that its practice was unscriptural. In the early years of their ecumenical involvement Disciples regularly identified themselves with the "free churches." Though they have come to recognize some of their most characteristic practices as "catholic," held in common with Anglicans, Romans, and Orthodox, most of them feel stronger bonds of temperament with the "leftwing" traditions historically committed to personal and religious liberty. The first number of *The Christian-Evangelist* for 1948 featured a box setting forth in bold type excerpts from the "Manifesto on Religious Freedom" issued by the Baptist World Alliance, and in a paper on "The Contributions of Separatism to American Life," Howard Elmo Short devoted several paragraphs to "The Baptists and Religious Liberty."[7]

The divisions among Disciples have been perceived as issuing from the struggle for freedom. In the separation between Churches of Christ and Disciples of Christ, the former resisted the innovations, especially the rise of "ecclesiasticism" and the latter acted in the belief that they were free to adopt expedients concerning which the Scriptures were silent. In the more recent parting which separated the undenominational fellowship of Christian Churches and Churches of Christ from the Christian Church (Disciples of Christ), the fear of ecclesiastical structure motivated the former, while the latter moved toward an ecclesiology which gave them freedom to act together "as church." Within the latter group, the liberal reformulation of the "Plea" which occurred early in the century made much of freedom. Two of the great liberal historians of the movement resisted latter-day trends which they found threatening. W. E. Garrison, in company with many old line liberals, continued a forthright opposition to creeds, and in the discussion of the proposal for bishops in the historic succession advanced by the Consultation on Church Union, A. T. DeGroot produced vigorous pamphlets on the negative side. Despite their reservations, however, posited on the classic Disciple understanding of freedom, these persons continued a loyal identity with the restructured church.[8] We shall return to issues involved in restructure at a later point. Here we simply note that liberty has been a dominant theme and a continuing disposition with Disciples.

The Movement's Three-Part Formula

Twentieth century Disciples have tended to interpret their venture as a movement for Christian unity, while an earlier generation more commonly referred to it as the Restoration Movement. Independent Christian Churches and the Churches of Christ still emphasize the vocabulary of "restoration." Historians have been inclined to link these two concerns: the founders sought to achieve Christian unity through restoration, or they set out to restore primitive Christianity as a goal, but with the confidence that it would eventuate in the union of Christians. My own study of the Declaration and Address convinces me that union and restoration are inextricably intertwined in the thought of Thomas Campbell. In my opinion, union was the dominant motivation of Barton W. Stone with restoration a self-evident means, while Alexander Campbell and Walter Scott first found themselves attracted to restoration and later added the interest in union.

However one may interpret the interrelationship between these two concerns, one oversimplifies by focusing only on them. The venture was more complex.

Liberty was part of the formula from the start. Sometimes explicitly, always implicitly, it entered into the articulations of the position, and in most cases it was a more potent motivation than either of the other two. It interests me that though in his formal writings as a historian W. E. Garrison relies on the unity-restoration polarity, nevertheless his more personal or confessional statements include liberty as an essential element in the position. In discussing "Why I Continue to be a Disciple," he mentioned "three specific points about the Christian Churches which make them congenial to my spirit":[9]

> *First, they hold and teach the essentials of Christianity. . . . [This is how a religious liberal formulates the restoration motif.]*
> *Second, they recognize the liberty of the Christian man and permit great freedom in thought and practice.*
> *Third, on the basis of a Christ-centered faith and the utmost freedom in all controversial details, they plead for the unity of Christians in the One Church. There is no other basis for a true and desirable unity.*

Throughout this series of lectures I have been pressing the thesis that the concern for liberty is an original and essential part of the Disciple formulation. Founders and successors alike included it as a major commitment equal in importance with any other. They subscribed to the ideal of political liberty. They valued personal liberty. Most particularly as a religious movement they undertook to secure liberty in the church. Some of them insisted on it for themselves more forcefully than they undertook to guarantee it to others. But always it was part of their program, even when they violated it in particular observance.

The history of Disciples is in large measure a story of interaction among the three commitments—unity, restoration, liberty—with a shift from time to time of one or another into the position of dominance. So interrelated were they in the mind of Disciples that one cannot adequately discuss any of the three apart from the other two. It is quite clear that we can understand neither unity nor restoration as they conceived it unless we emphasize the component of liberty which they saw in it.

The impulse toward Christian unity led both Barton Stone and Thomas Campbell to insist on practicing unity even though that involved the paradox of their separation from the Presbyterian Church. Their whole program was one to enable God's people to "go free," and to that end they appealed to the practice of the primitive church. Enter restoration.

To many American intellectuals from Thomas Jefferson on through the first half of the nineteenth century, the notion of returning to primitive simplicity was the self-evident way to

88

freedom and virtue. Alexander Campbell simply applied the prevailing mindset to the life of the church when he began "to contend for the original faith and order in opposition to all the corruptions of fifteen centuries" left as stumbling blocks on the roadway of freedom. Restoration served as a liberating principle, removing the stumbling blocks—"the rubbish of ages"— so that Christians could advance unhampered by the restraints of autocracy and superstition. Thus it also opened a freeway to unity, rid of the obstructions of old sectarianism. In time, Disciples lost the realization of the bond which united liberty and union with restoration. The "ancient order of things" became an end in itself, particularly when their study of the New Testament led them to insist exclusively on the immersion of believers as the only acceptable baptism. Restoration then became a principle of division, with liberty on this issue severely curtailed (though never denied among the churches which continued the tradition of Barton Stone).[10]

In the middle generation, restoration was a self-evident value, elevated to a position of dominance, and a Disciple legalism of the Book fashioned an "iron bedstead"—a true irony of history!—not of creedalism but of "bibleism." Even so, the principle continued to exert some liberating power. In the controversy over open communion, Disciples happily found the verse which reads, "Let a man examine himself" (I Cor. 11:28), and though no one among them would grant for a moment the possibility of an unimmersed person's coming to the Lord's supper in apostolic times, a literal appeal to that verse allowed them to follow their hearts rather than their heads, to practice at the table an ecumenism they did not practice at the church door. Later on the intellectuals among them undertook to formulate a rationale for their position which sounded less legalistic. W. T. Moore, Peter Ainslie, F. D. Kershner spoke of the catholic witness of Disciples—a catholic creed (the Petrine Confession), a catholic baptism (recognized by all), a catholic table (not closed to any believer), a catholic name (Christian). The term *catholic* was hardly one to inspire great popular acclaim among Disciples, but it was pressed into service as a means of liberation from the legalism which had overtaken the concept of restoration.[11]

In the early twentieth century, widespread acceptance of the myth of progress and a different view of the early church which came with the work of biblical scholars engaged in historical criticism and form-criticism cut the ground of plausibility from under the old concept of restoration. Increasing numbers of Disciples muted it or abandoned it altogether in favor of a larger emphasis on unity and liberty; if it survived it was in some such form as Garrison's emphasis on "the essentials of Christianity." With the Churches of Christ and the "independent" Christian Churches restoration remained a commitment undiminished in emphasis.[12]

Report on the Experiment

Meanwhile, in the days when all Disciples professed allegiance to the entire triad (unity, restoration, liberty), they had institutionalized in their churchly life certain mechanisms of freedom. These were anti-clericalism, anti-creedalism, and anti-ecclesiasticism. By means of these mechanisms they undertook to secure liberty in the church. Each of these negative positions, moreover, became a powerful symbolic force in the ethos of Disciples, no less among liberals than among traditionalists. To them all, clergy, creeds, and church-courts were interrelated distortions in the Christianity of the denominations. These aberrations inhibited freedom, shattered unity, and contravened the practice of the apostolic church.

It is now time to proceed to our second consideration. How has the Disciples' experiment in liberty turned out? We shall examine their experience with each of their three mechanisms of freedom.

Anti-clericalism

In the iconoclastic days of his early leadership, Alexander Campbell led a spirited revolt against the "kingdom of the clergy." The sarcasm he directed against the "hireling priests" resulted in some of the most colorful, even demagogic language that ever issued from his pen. In his putdown of the official guardians of orthodoxy and rectitude in the oldline churches Campbell appealed mightily to the predispositions of frontier Americans. He heaped his scorn upon pretentious ignorance, as among some frontier Baptists, or pretentious learning, as among some Presbyterians. He ridiculed preaching for pay. He lampooned the lordship of bishops, and he turned from humor to white-hot anger in excoriating the claims of the Roman hierarchy. (In his attitude toward episcopacy and papacy he remained a child of Ulster.) This sort of anti-clericalism was by no means unique with Campbell or with Disciples. The diatribes of the famed Methodist circuit-rider Peter Cartwright against the learned ineptitude of graduates from Eastern seminaries matched Campbell's for quality and flavor. The

Cumberland Presbyterians arose in the same region and among the same type of persons as did Disciples, rebelling not against an ordered ministry as such, but against what seemed unnecessary complexities of doctrine and irrelevant requirements for theological education.[13]

Campbell advanced a doctrine of ministry, already mentioned in connection with the service of the congregation to personal liberty, based on "the ancient order of things." This "standing and immutable ministry" of the Christian community, he maintained, was that of evangelists, elders (he preferred to call them bishops), and deacons. The office of evangelist claimed such educated preachers as Disciples had until late in the nineteenth century. Not to be confused with high-pressure, professional revivalists, they were unpretentious, hard-working men who gave what time they could spare from earning a living to itinerating the countryside, preaching the gospel, baptizing converts, gathering congregations, and "setting churches in order." This last transaction required two conditions. First, a local company of believers needed a sufficient number of members to constitute themselves by covenant as a church of Christ. Second, they must have among them at least two men who met the scriptural qualifications for elders. Turning the new church over to the care of these "pastors and teachers," the evangelist withdrew from his informal superintendency over the congregation and went on his way rejoicing.[14]

The elders or bishops now charged with the "rule" of the congregation continued to earn their living at their secular vocations, receiving no pay for their ministry. (The evangelists had received precious little.) They presided, not singly but by pairs, at the Lord's table, and one of them would "speak" or "teach" at the service of worship. The deacons, also local men, rarely carried duties which other traditions reserved for ministers, though Campbell tried hard to present their work of caring for the needy and helping in other ways as an office of ministry. In later times, elders and deacons formed "the board of officers" in the church, transacting its business except for such major items as required formal action by the congregation. But in the earlier years democracy did not always prevail in church government. The congregation elected its elders, ordaining them "for life"—or at least for the duration of their membership in that place. The elders then "ruled," on the basis of office. Younger people often resented their authoritarian ways. Even so, the elders never thought of themselves as clergy, comparable to the ministers of the denominations. Rather, they constituted the ministry authorized by the New

Testament, and they led the congregation in the "breaking of bread" every Lord's Day.

After the Civil War, the growth of the churches, especially in the cities, led to a demand for fulltime, better educated pastors, and the good preachers began to settle down. Despite the cry that evangelists ought to itinerate and that the "one-man system" was unscriptural, the pattern grew. Today it prevails in all the wings of the movement, even though no one ever really justified it in restoration terms. For a long time the theory prevailed that "the pastor" was one of the elders. In the 1880s it was still common for the minister to use Elder as his official title. A sharp controversy arose when some ministers accepted the designation "Reverend," and it has been only in the past two decades that Disciples generally have given up total abstinence in this matter.

Whatever their theories, the pragmatic common sense of Disciples told them that they needed fulltime pastoral leadership, and they got it. Programs of ministerial education expanded, until today graduation from seminary is standard expectation for ordination.

During the early decades of this century a power struggle went on within congregations between the minister and the elders. The ministers won by persuading the congregations to adopt the principle of stated terms, with rotation, for service by elders and deacons. Most Disciples now speak of eldership as a lay office, rather than an office of ministry. Yet the elders continue to offer the prayers of thanksgiving at the Lord's table, even if increasingly in the role of assistants to the minister, who presides. During the past decade growing numbers of congregations have elected women as well as men to the eldership and the diaconate.

The Christian Church (Disciples of Christ) now recognizes an "order of the ministry" made up of ordained and licensed ministers whose standing is certified by the church in the region. Many of these refer to themselves as "clergy" in order to affirm their status as professionals; they tend to interpret this status as deriving from education and recognized expertise rather than from sacramental character.[15]

The general policy of the church declares the office of ministry open both to women and to men, even though a few biblical literalists continue to quote Scripture against women's eligibility to serve as ministers or elders. Disciples have ordained women for some time; a quarter of a century ago one of the best known of these, Mossie Allman Wyker, published an informed argument in favor of the practice. If the congregations have been slow to call women ministers to responsible posts, a gradual change seems to be under way.[16]

For the most part Disciples have perceived their passage from anti-clericalism as part of their "growing up" as a denomination and not as a serious threat to freedom. During the rampant anti-institutionalism of the 1960s something of that mood combined with popular slogans concerning the ministry of the laity left over from the previous decade to produce a flash of rhetoric downgrading the "clergy." That appears to have subsided. Occasionally lay persons on the losing side in an action taken at the General Assembly complain that the preachers have too many votes, but analysis has discovered no issue which lined up ministers on one side and lay persons on the other. Procedures of the church provide for balance on general boards and committees—equal numbers of women with men, and a proportion of ministers somewhere between one-third and one-half of the total number.

Three questions concerning the ministry remain unresolved:

(1) What is the eldership today? Despite efforts (in early discussions on restructure and in the Consultation on Church Union) to reaffirm Campbell's doctrine of eldership as an order of ministry, most Disciples have not responded positively. They see eldership as a lay office and so infer that the presidency at the table is a function open to lay persons. Yet in ordinary circumstances the minister presides. More of this later.

(2) What is the essential character of ordained ministry? Apparently many do not perceive it sacramentally, but rather in terms of professional education and job assignment. Church management has become a major element in defining the role. And the unplanned pressures emanating from congregational concern for institutional success and from the promotional program of the denomination almost force ministers into the managerial mold. Church members used to speak of "calling" a minister; now they more commonly talk of "hiring" one.[17]

(3) How shall the freedom of the ministry be safeguarded among Disciples? The most authoritarian of Protestant structures, that of the United Methodist Church, protects the minister against irresponsible action by the congregation and against loss of employment. The Presbyterian system provides a counterweight against unilateral action by congregation or minister; in contrast with current Disciple procedure, it also grants a minister freedom to apply directly for a vacant pulpit.

Disciples no longer hurl about the anticlerical clichés in which they once delighted. They have accepted an order of ministry, even a professional clergy, and they perceive it as no

93

threat to their freedom—perhaps because in a showdown the congregation holds all the chips. They have reaped the benefits, but they have not yet secured the liberty of their ministers. This is a far more serious situation than the mere violation of the rights and privileges of an occasional "employee," sacred as those ought to be. To whatever extent any part of the church restricts the full freedom of a person appointed to minister the gospel of God, it hampers the whole church in fulfilling its vocation. Whenever a minister loses a position by the unilateral action of one congregation or institution, the entire body participates both in the guilt for any injustice done to one ordained in its name, and in the loss, temporary or permanent, of service from one whom it has nurtured, educated, and brought to usefulness. Disciples can no longer afford this irresponsibility, which lingers as a vestige of anticlericalism.

Anti-Creedalism

Both Stone and the Campbells struck repeated blows against creeds, in order to secure Christian liberty for the believer. Freedom of opinion was in the air. Rationalism and pietism converged to deprecate the policing of orthodoxy in fine points of doctrine. The mood of toleration which had been growing in society through the eighteenth century had begun to commend itself inside the church as well.[18]

Many of the doctrines spelled out in the historic confessions seemed to Disciples to violate common sense. Thus Stone had difficulty with the classical formulations concerning the Trinity and the atonement; to him they were speculations lacking in biblical foundation. Alexander Campbell dismissed such doctrines as "opinionism" and against them he opposed the true "bibleism." The only verbal formula to which Disciples required assent was Peter's confession: Thou art the Christ, the Son of the living God. Walter Scott termed it the Golden Oracle.[19]

The downgrading of human speculation extended from creeds and confessions to include the whole theological enterprise. Systems of thought which went beyond the evident teaching of Scripture (presumed to be clear and uniform throughout) were dismissed as confusing and lacking in value. So Alexander Campbell wrote into the charter of Bethany College a provision prohibiting the teaching of theology. Yet he conducted daily lectures on the Bible which all students were required to attend.

In time, however, an accepted line began to prevail among Disciples as to the essence of biblical teaching. They liked to talk about "first principles"—those essentials on which unity was expected. These included the "steps of salvation" (traced out by Walter Scott, but credited to the New Testament), the immersion of believers as the only true baptism, the weekly "breaking of bread," the sole propriety of biblical names for the church, the rejection of human creeds, and the union of Christians on the basis of these essentials. Holding strong convictions on these points, they found it hard to tolerate even a minor divergence as legitimate opinion. Conscientious elders set forth the truth on these matters with precision and carefully analyzed every sermon for orthodoxy. Young preachers were expected to be able to propound "first principles" at the drop of a hat and took pride in readiness to preach on any of the conversions in the New Testament at a moment's notice. Of course, such a limited diet grew tedious. From Washington, Congressman Garfield wrote to Hinsdale that he was fed up:

Wearied with the perpetual iteration of the doctrinal points of Bro. A.—and the intolerable denominational bigotry, arrogance, and egotism, with which he puts forth the formal parts of 'our plea,' I went this morning to hear a Swedenborgian and am glad I did so.

Many other listeners also grew tired of such preaching, and young ministers wearied of having to trace the same old rut in every sermon.[20]

Nevertheless the heritage of anticreedalism proved to be a guarantor of liberty for the more liberal ministers at the turn of the century, particularly as they disentangled that heritage from biblicism and linked it with a positive commitment to the spirit of Christ. The liberal restructuring of the Disciple position naturally played up the anti-creedal stance. In cases where charges of heresy were brought against professors or missionaries, it provided a telling appeal for freedom. And the historian must conclude that without benefit of creed, Disciples strayed no farther from orthodoxy in the Modernist era than did those denominations which officially subscribed to creeds.[21]

In the 1950s, when the voice of neoorthodoxy was heard in the land, numbers of churches exercised their freedom by introducing unison affirmations of faith into worship. (Even earlier, some had used compilations of biblical passages in this way.) During the process of restructure, Dean Blakemore's Committee on Fundamental Documents compiled an impressive body of confessional materials which Disciples were using liturgically. And the affirmation which introduces the Preamble to the "Provisional Design for the Christian Church (Disciples of Christ)" frequently occurs in orders of worship. Most Disciples registered no difficulty with the COCU proposal in "A Plan of Union" that the Church of Christ Uniting will "use" the Apostle's Creed and Nicene Creed as "classic expressions of the Christian faith," and not as tests of fellowship.[22]

Some persons at the extreme left, as at the extreme right have appealed to the anti-creedal heritage in protesting "official" or corporate statements describing what Disciples believe. One of the deepest instincts within them all opposes any coercive use of creeds. Yet Disciples sometimes confess a sense of theological inadequacy owing to their lack of a confessional tradition. Many are concluding that perhaps creeds are not entirely bad. In a time of widespread biblical ignorance, when the presuppositions of the culture threaten to engulf the church, many Disciples welcome the freedom of the people of God to proclaim their corporate faith and to teach it through creeds both old and new.

Anti-Ecclesiasticism

It was trouble with ecclesiastical courts that led both Stone and Thomas Campbell to withdraw from the Presbyterian connection. Young Alexander's disturbance over procedures for admitting or excluding members from holy communion led him to the same step. Soon he was inveighing against ecclesiastical authorities of all kinds as violating the freedom of Christians and lacking scriptural warrant. The fervid rhetoric of iconoclasm published in *The Christian Baptist* pulled the new movement in a direction Campbell did not foresee. It parallels a cowboy's experience in Texas fifty years later, narrated by Captain Henry of Geauga, for the old folks at home in Ohio:

He was under the influence of animal and other spirits one day when an engine came along going slowly up a grade. The cowboy had lassoed many a heavy steer; he sighed for more worlds or more steers to conquer. His face lighted with inspiration and firm resolve, he mounted his horse, and with the speed of the wind he overtook the laboring engine. Whiz went the lasso and round and round the smokestack went the end. He had caught it fast and now came the tug of war. The horse braced, the rope came taut, and in an instant horse and cowboy were in a confused heap dragging along beside the track under the influence and power of civilization. The engineer, being good-natured, stopped and cut the lasso near the saddle, keeping the longest end for a trophy, invited the cowboy to try again, pulled the throttle, and moved onward.[23]

96

Something similar happened when Campbell and his Reformers lassoed the locomotive of anti-ecclesiasticism, except that no compassionate engineer stopped to cut the rope. For a long time that big, chuffing iron horse dragged them bruised but determined across the desert of independency. It began in 1830 when, to Campbell's consternation, Walter Scott offered the motion to dissolve the Mahoning Baptist Association, which the Reformers clearly dominated. Before Campbell could speak against the motion, it had carried, and the first institutional base for the New Reformation had been destroyed. After a decade of trying to lead a company of independent congregations, Campbell began to agitate for a general church organization. Even so, the first general convention, called in 1849 as an assembly of delegates from the congregations, turned itself into a mass meeting. One hundred and twenty years would pass before Disciples would accept an ecclesiastical structure.[24]

The repudiation of ecclesiasticism included an attack upon denominations as such. In the view of Disciples, the sects had splintered over inconsequential issues: "There is no salvation in the things that divide," said E. V. Zollars. To make matters worse, they had organized synods, conferences, and other such unscriptural authorities to enforce their petty orthodoxies and control their ministers, thus keeping simple Christians apart. The original strategy of Disciples for Christian union was the dissolution of all ecclesiastical structures, as they had disposed of the Mahoning Baptist Association. When the various denominational instruments of power had been removed from the scene, nothing would be left but free congregations no longer divided by creed or ecclesiastical fiat. Once persuaded to drop their partisan names and to follow only the New Testament as their rule of faith and practice, they would enter the golden age. Christian unity was defined as the liquidation of denominational structure and identity. Since Disciples were leading the way, they insisted with great fervor, "We are not a denomination."[25]

Yet Disciples learned that the elimination of ecclesiastical machinery did not restore them to a paradise of innocence and freedom. Alexander Campbell, for example, traveled to Nashville to put pressure on the church there to remove Jesse B. Ferguson, whose Spiritualism, Universalism, and general style of leadership troubled him. Granted that Campbell could not have got rid of the preacher except by strengthening the opposition within the congregation. Still his departure would not likely have followed without such intervention, and Ferguson naturally felt himself to have been ill used. Even within "free congregations" petty dictators arose. In the nineteenth century these were generally elders intent on maintaining their notions of what was "essential" according to Scripture and hence outside the realm of liberty. In the twentieth century some ministers succeeded in running their churches like autocrats, and an occasional "big giver" tried to do so.[26]

The very lack of structure—some called it anarchy—also impinged on freedom. From the earliest days of the movement, a need was felt to prevent the foisting upon the brotherhood of unprepared and unworthy evangelists ordained unilaterally by single congregations. But whether proposals looking toward more responsible procedure came before a state or a general convention, fear of ecclesiasticism caused Disciples to back off. At last, in the mid-twentieth century, successful cooperation between state commissions on the ministry and sponsoring congregations, prepared the way for one of the significant advances in restructure. "A Provisional Design" authorizes the General Assembly to establish policies and procedures regarding the ministry and vests the regions with responsibility for certification of standing.[27]

The lack of ecclesiastical machinery also hampered the freedom of Disciples for full and responsible ecumenical participation. Resorting to a mode of action that had become standard, a group of interested persons at the National Convention of 1907 called a special mass meeting. Acting as individuals, the participants voted to enter into the Federal Council of Churches and to authorize representatives. Even after the International Convention of Disciples of Christ (constituted in 1917) took over responsibility for authorizing ecumenical delegations, they tended to speak with diffidence. In effect, they said, they could express personal opinion, which they believed to be representative, but "no one can speak for the Disciples." I myself wrote something like that—because we are a "free people"—in our *Response to Lund,* published in 1953. The following summer I met with the Union Committee of the Churches of Christ [Disciples] in Great Britain. They gave me a bad time about that statement. "It may be that no one can speak for American Disciples," they said, "but if so, you are not free."[28]

The developments which led to restructure and the constitution of the Christian Church (Disciples of Christ) made evident the paradoxical character of the anti-ecclesiastical heritage. In their witness to liberty, the founders had planted their feet in opposition to denominational organization. In the experience of their children, however, congregational independence did not

98

always make for freedom. So both the proponents and the opponents of restructure took their positions in accordance with their commitment to freedom. And, as we shall see, after a while the Provisional Design for restructure provided general ecclesiastical relationships while continuing to guarantee personal and congregational liberty.

Before leaving the issue of anti-ecclesiasticism, it must be noted that this mechanism, operating in the form of congregational and personal independence, did operate to secure important freedoms for Disciples. It allowed for the voluntary spread of new practices as individual congregations approved them. The introduction of musical instruments in worship is one example; of course, it proved so offensive to some preachers and congregations that they refused to continue fellowship with the "digressives." The practice of open membership is another example. Disciples had no effective way of preventing congregations from adopting this policy; opposition to it was an emotional factor, but not the deciding one, in the development of the second major schism. In general, congregational polity favored the growth of liberalism among Disciples in the decades before and after the turn of the century. Most of them at that time were stoutly conservative. With fear and conviction they resisted liberal thought. As a rule, the liberals were gifted persons, educated well beyond the average. So long as one of them could find or found a congregation to provide support, no one else in the brotherhood had authority to interfere. Many would like to have seen the liberals leave; some would have thrown them out if they had had the power. But the liberals proved that anyone who wanted to stay with the brotherhood had freedom to do so, assuming of course that a means of financial support could be found.[29]

Moreover, the principle of responsible voluntarism enabled Disciples to develop a remarkably dynamic program of cooperative activities. When Campbell's proposed general church organization based on representation lost out at Cincinnati in 1849, the Disciples gathered there constituted both the general convention as an annual mass meeting (open to any member of a Christian Church) and the missionary society as a body of individuals. Thus even though they could not permit any "church organization," holding that there was no such thing except in the form of the congregation, they did launch an organization of Disciples to carry out the mission which Christ had laid upon all his followers. Unlike the founders of early journals and colleges, however, the officers of the missionary society reported annually on their work to a general meeting of its members. In subsequent years, additional societies were formed, each with a specific purpose, and the general convention became a sequence of annual meetings of these various "agencies," held in the same place on successive days and attended by essentially the same people. In time, cries for greater cooperation and coordination arose—in matters of calendar, program, publication, budget, and review. The succession of annual meetings gave way in 1917 to the International Convention of Disciples of Christ—a bicameral meeting with two houses: the Committee on Recommendations composed of delegates from state conventions, and the Assembly which was still a mass meeting. The growing dependence of the agencies on the approval (moral, not legal) of the convention, and their ever deeper mutual involvements in budgeting and program coordination led to the pragmatic demand for restructure. At the same time the realization that the work being done by the agencies was the mission of the church, not just of individual Christians, pushed Disciples toward the deepening of their ecclesiology.[30]

A landmark in the development of Disciple thinking about the church was the development in the 1950s of the "Strategy of World Missions." It was a response to the maturing of the "younger churches" and to the intense discussion in ecumenical circles of their proper relationship with the churches in Europe and America, whose missionary efforts had brought them into being. Demands were heard for the emancipation of the churches in Asia and Africa from their status as "missions" controlled by the "sending churches," for their right to request fraternal workers rather than just receive missionaries chosen by someone else, for control of Christian institutions and properties in their own lands, and for the right to negotiate for church union free from the threat of domination or veto on the part of the boards in the West. As chairman of the World Division of the United Christian Missionary Society, Virgil A. Sly organized a series of "listening conferences" across the United States and Canada. Hundreds of Disciples from the grassroots took part in these meetings, considering the issues and freely expressing their opinions. Out of these discussions, a consensus began to emerge, resulting in the adoption of a major policy document. It took seriously in this new situation the implications of "the fundamental New Testament principle of congregational form of church government," recognizing the right of the churches overseas to take decisions "without autocratic control" by Americans who might not always agree with the actions. The adoption of the "strategy" document ended an era of paternalism in missions. The process leading to it also deepened the understanding of American and Canadian Disciples concerning the nature of the church and the meaning of Christian freedom.[31]

The proponents of so-called "independent" missions adopted the principle of individual initiative without providing any corresponding mechanism for responsible oversight by the brotherhood at large. The independent missionaries sent accounts of their work directly to their sponsors or to journals which would publish them. They traveled among their supporting churches and met their colleagues at the ("independent") North American Christian Convention, but this assembly conducted no business and exercised no oversight. The entire appeal was to freedom.[32]

All Disciples remained highly sensitive with respect to the rights and freedoms of congregations. The greatest journalistic stir I can recall over any issue during my lifetime followed the publication of an article in *The Christian-Evangelist* by Barnett Blakemore in 1953 entitled "Autonomy? NO! Independency? YES!" Arguing that autonomy was an unbiblical concept and a term not used regarding congregations until after 1910, Dean Blakemore held that it was a fallacious notion clouding the sole lordship of Christ over his church. What it meant to assert that was right was the proper independency of congregations from ecclesiastical overlordship. For months afterwards nervous responses and refutations poured into the editorial offices.[33]

Fifteen years later as the time to vote on "A Provisional Design" drew near it became evident that its adoption hinged on the inclusion of specific reference to the "integrity, self-government, rights and responsibilities" of congregations (as well as other "manifestations") of the Christian Church. The Commission on Restructure affirmed such freedoms both theologically and legally without the use of the term "autonomy." Later, when the member churches in the Consultation on Church Union were studying "A Plan of Union for the Church of Christ Uniting," hundreds of congregations, agencies, and individuals among the Disciples responded in writing. Relatively little discomfort was expressed at the prospect of bishops in the united church but the responses were overwhelming in their opposition to the requirement that congregations surrender the ownership of their property to the new COCU parish. The congregational control of its property remains an important symbol of freedom to most Disciples of Christ.[34]

101

Results of the Experiment

In summary, we may observe that Disciples in their experiment in churchly freedom adopted three mechanisms for the guarantee of liberty: anti-clericalism, anti-creedalism, anti-ecclesiasticism. At the beginning, the opposition was dogmatic to the point of absolutism. Across a century and a half of experiment, their common-sense assessment of their own experience and their initiative as free spirits led Disciples to significant revision of the original position. They developed an order of ministry working under policies and procedures of the general and regional church. They made increasing use of creeds and affirmations of faith in worship. They worked out an ecclesiastical structure founded on a larger ecclesiology than they had at first and regulated by a constitutional document. Yet devotion to the freedom which the original mechanisms were intended to secure remains as strong as ever. The Christian Church (Disciples of Christ) is not ruled by a clergy, nor can it be under its procedures. It makes no creedal test of fellowship beyond the affirmation of faith in Jesus Christ as Lord. It has no instrument of power to control the life of its congregations. The commitment to churchly liberty remains.

Resources for Freedom
in a United Church

At present, Christians are speaking with less certainty about the form of the church in the future than characterized much ecumenical utterance a few years ago. Will a united church emerge on the scale envisioned by the Consultation on Church Union? Will Disciples move shortly to a union with the United Church of Christ? Will present denominational structures continue as useful instruments of program and tradition while local and regional clusters, councils, and conferences of churches become far more prominent instruments of unity than they have been? Will the churches fall back into a renewed dominance of localism and congregational independence? One cannot answer such questions today with much assurance. Nevertheless I continue to believe in and to labor for the hastening of that time when Disciples no longer continue as a separate people but, finding a larger freedom in a united church, may share with others their experiment in liberty.

Without thinking of their distinctive practices as demands to be made upon others but rather as the choicest fruits of their experience, Disciples might well commend from their history a cluster of emphases closely related to their love of freedom.

The Centrality and Supremacy of Christ in His Church

To affirm that Jesus Christ is Lord is to confess the reconciling power of him who unites all who name his name. Disciples may lay claim to no superior devotion to him, no unique insight into his will for his church, no peculiar recognition of his preeminence. Nevertheless they may rightly interpret the thrust of their history as an effort to affirm his dominion in all things, both through the positive procedures they adopted and through the rejection of certain longstanding ecclesiastical practices, so that Christians might know the freedom for which Christ set them free. Barton Stone, Thomas and Alexander Campbell, Walter Scott, Robert Richardson, Charles Louis Loos, E. V. Zollars, Peter Ainslie, and many others since have made the "Golden Oracle" central in Christian faith.

Some years ago, coming across a sentence which F. D. Maurice, the celebrated Anglican theologian wrote in 1838, Dean W. B. Blakemore commended it in an article which he entitled "Campbell Out-Campbellited." The sentence runs as follows:

The Church is a body united in the acknowledgment of a living Person; *every sect is a body united in the acknowledgment of a certain* notion.

Dean Blakemore asks, "Was there ever a more accurate way of stating just what Campbell wished to say?" Campbell maintained that he could not discover an instance in history showing "that one single person was either converted or sanctified by memorizing any catechism, heterodox or orthodox." Creeds and catechisms deal in notions. He insisted on the Bible as the basic textbook for Christians precisely because it bears witness to the *person* Jesus Christ. The point is made graphic by a diagram a pastor sent me nearly twenty years ago under the title "CHRIST CENTERED RELIGION." At the center is a circle inscribed around a cross. Overlapping and reaching out from it like malformed petals about the disk of a daisy is a series of narrow elipses. Each of these overlaps the others only slightly; for the most part it is separate because it has *two* foci, the cross *and* some other emphasis—creed, doctrine, church, method, name, etc. The interpretation of the diagram suggests that division among Christians has resulted from undue emphasis on one or another of these secondary centers, that the way to Christian unity (and the plea of Disciples) is to restore

103

the church to its original purpose by again making Christ the center of its life.[35]

In this time of increasing dialog among the various world religions a new syncretism, which some mistakenly label ecumenism, appeals to many. Without going into this issue deeply, it is possible to say two things. First, Jesus Christ includes in his redemptive love every human being. I believe he calls all who name his name to openness toward all spiritual truth and to the gracious acceptance of all other persons whatever their faith. Second, Christians cannot accept for themselves situations which seem to place the founders of the various religions on the same level. (In the Bahai Temple at Wilmette, Illinois I saw the Christian gallery, along with others, flanking the central vault. In a Spiritualist garden at Chesterfield, Indiana I walked among pedestals displaying busts of Ikhnaton, Moses, Confucius, Gautama Buddha, Jesus, Mohammed, and others.) As Christians we honor the teachers of various faiths, but we hold them subordinate to Christ. As much as we may learn from other religions, we do not regard them as equal to the gospel. To us Christ is supreme.

Christian freedom is inseparable from covenant-allegiance to Jesus Christ as Lord. Acknowledging him as the Way, the Truth, and the Life, believers voluntarily give themselves to him. Yet, writes Lin D. Cartwright,

It is . . . one of the strange paradoxes of the Christian faith that when once the authority of Christ is freely accepted, the Christian experiences instead of shackles and restraint a new liberating sense of freedom and release.

The life of discipleship is the freedom of a crew holding a vessel to its course despite changeable winds and seas and so arriving safe at port in contrast with the apparent liberty of a company who let their ship drift with every current. Much that passes for freedom today is simply the striking of all standards and giving way to self-permissiveness before any impulse. But if the secular mind has difficulty with lordship as the perfect law of liberty, many religious people have been discontent with a gospel which maintains the sufficiency of Christ's grace. The apostle Paul was accused of antinomianism because he based salvation on that grace rather than on keeping a set of moral rules, and Thomas Campbell was charged with latitudinarianism because he accepted faith in Christ and did not demand theological agreement on the "many inferential truths" about fine points of doctrine, which many did not understand. Disciples have contended for the sufficiency of Christ.[36]

It is precisely when Christ is made supreme that he frees and unites. Charles Clayton Morrison was asked to contribute to a discussion, "Why I Am a Disciple." The climax of his response runs as follows:

... *the fathers themselves had something better to offer as a basis of union than their interpretation of certain features of the New Testament church. Insistently they proclaimed Jesus Christ as the basis of union. Faith in his divine Lordship was the sole test of membership in the true church. All else was "opinion," in which realm Christians enjoyed liberty. ...*

It is this liberty which I appropriate to myself as a Disciple. In this liberty to hold and express my disagreements with my brethren in the realm of opinion I find a fellowship unconstrained, because I know that, below our disagreements, we share a common and unifying faith in the one Lord, who is the sole Head of the church which is his Body.

Disciples have undertaken to respond seriously to the centrality and supremacy of Jesus Christ in his church. The insight from their experience with that principle they bring to the church of the future.[37]

A Commitment to Normative Christianity

In launching their "current Reformation" for the union of Christians, the early Disciples advanced a method which they epitomized as "the restoration of primitive Christianity." Sometimes in their writings and often in the practice of the middle generation, this came out as pure "New Testamentism" or textual literalism. At other times their language, if not their attitude, sounded more open, as in Alexander Campbell's reference to "the apostolic platform of church union, communion, and cooperation" or to "the original faith and order." Their intention was clear enough—to discard all non-essential requirements for fellowship in the one church and to concentrate on the life-giving essentials. Their appeal to the New Testament, even though distorted by literalistic presuppositions which many find no longer tenable, was designed to serve that intention. This preoccupation with the Bible as a rule did on occasion provide a means of emancipation from a dry and constricted Christian experience. Archibald McLean, for example, aroused Disciples from parochialism to a concern for worldwide witness by his biblically inspired missionary vision. His addresses proved remarkably persuasive and authentic in no small measure because of the appeal which their title derived from the old slogan: *Where the Book Speaks.* Later Disciples have found a return to the sacred text a means of liberation from racism, sexism, and other exclusive attitudes.[38]

Disciples (here distinguished from members of the Churches of Christ and of the "independent" Christian Churches) have generally abandoned those notions of restoration which supposed the New Testament to contain a blue-print for every aspect of the church's life and organization. Yet in the midst of historical relativism and cultural pluralism, the church needs to center on the essentials of the faith in such a way as to secure both integrity and liberty. It requires a surer sense of direction than that of an aimless company of free spirits improvising whatever patterns of thought or action seem attractive at the moment. Walter Sikes, George Beazley, Barnett Blakemore, and others were able to work out a mature biblical theology, as William Robinson had done before them. That mode of doing theology is not so much in vogue now as it was two decades ago. But the memory of the original devotion to restorationism, however inadequately it may have been stated, remains with Disciples in a continuing concern to "search the Scriptures."

Disciples realize that they will not discover normative Christianity by trying to "go it alone." Instead, they mean to approach the Bible in company with other Christians, open to all the insights of contemporary scholarship and aware of the total Christian tradition. By a process of honest interaction between the contemporary mind and the biblical witness they would avoid the old primitivism and at the same time escape engulfment by the culture. In my own judgment, the church of the future must give larger attention to the norms of its life in concern for the full-orbed wholeness of the Christian faith than has been evident in the voguishness of recent years. Only such a church can find freedom to bear an authentic Christian witness.

Unity and Union—with Liberty

The search for unity with liberty is a dominant ecumenical concern at the moment, as the widespread discussion of diversity makes evident. In the formulation of W. E. Garrison, medieval Catholicism produced unity without liberty, Protestantism produced liberty without unity, the ecumenical task is the achievement of unity with liberty and liberty with unity. Ernst Troeltsch saw the dynamic of history working against unity and universality; rather the increasing growth of freedom would make for greater and greater diversity and individuality. Yet Disciples cannot evade their vocation. Despite the schisms in their own history, they believe that God wills the oneness of his people. They believe that emphasis on Jesus Christ provides the basis for Christian unity with the widest range of diversity and freedom.[39]

Two distinct concepts require mention here. One is unity among Christians. The other is church union. The former is primarily a matter of mutual recognition and the practice of charity. It is, I believe, the genius of Garrison's vision. With much greater intensity than at present, Christians will acknowledge one another, confer with one another, help one another, love one another, work with one another. It is a noble vision, obscured by few theoretical problems, its fulfilment delayed only by human perversity. It readily commends itself to the sentiments of those who confess Christ as Lord. The eloquence of Thomas Campbell powerfully exhorts Christians to the practice of such love. In Proposition 9 of the Declaration and Address, he submits

That all that are enabled, thro' grace, to make . . . a profession [of faith in Christ], and to manifest the reality of it in their tempers and conduct, should consider each other as the precious saints of God, should love each other as brethren, children of the same family and father, temples of the same spirit, members of the same body, subjects of the same grace, objects of the same divine love, bought with the same price, and joint heirs of the same inheritance. Whom God hath thus joined together no man should dare to put asunder.

Yet even among those who cherish in their hearts the love here celebrated the division of the churches operates to put them asunder.

Church union, as distinguished from unity among Christians, seeks to overcome institutional divisions. It is no easy process. It was not achieved by the early Disciple strategy of liquidating the denominations. The contemporary ecumenical effort to bring them together reckons seriously with the visible character of the church. Yet we must acknowledge that any institution is a historic artifact and consequently less than absolute. Because it seems highly unlikely that all Christians will agree on any conceivable institutional manifestation of the church, many continue to opt for "spiritual union" alone—what we have called unity among Christians. It is not to be despised. But neither is it sufficient if it in any way minimizes the reality and the visibility of the one church as an institution in history.

Along with most of the major communions, the Christian Church (Disciples of Christ) has committed itself to the faith that God is calling his people to a larger manifestation of church union than has yet been achieved, a union enriched by diversity and blessed with liberty. If Disciples have not settled all the issues involved in reaching that goal, they are nevertheless committed to it, and to the symbolic importance of continuing serious negotiations for union. In all such ventures they have undertaken (in words attributed to Peter Ainslie) to "hold sacred those values that are precious to other people."[40]

Disciples have found in their heritage what Hampton Adams called "a freedom to adventure in the ecumenical church." Certainly in many communities they have taken the lead in promoting movements toward union. They have provided a significant company of ecumenical leaders from Peter Ainslie to Paul Crow. They have given consistent and vigorous support to the Consultation on Church Union and to the maintenance of morale for that undertaking, even though some of its leaders at the start presumed that Disciples would not be able to participate. Through the action of their General Assembly in 1975 they responded to the request of the Consultation for an affirmation, along with the other participating churches, of the mutual recognition of members. Carried by an overwhelming vote, this action has occasioned far less objection than some had anticipated. Without claiming that they possess the solution to all the problems, Disciples are committed to Christian union with Christian freedom, and they believe that the goal can be achieved. In the words of William Robinson, they seek "the oneness of the visible church on the Pauline basis of liberty and corporate loyalty." And they rejoice that this concern is not theirs alone, but that it motivates Christians of many names in the ecumenical quest.[41]

The Tone and Shape of Worship

After some frustrating attempts to work out a precise and authoritative order of worship stipulated by the New Testament, early Disciples fell back into a situation of widespread liberty in the arrangement of the church's public services. In a general way, we may say that the prevailing pattern has passed through a number of stages, from early restorationist attempts, through the cold, spare order that emphasized "head religion," the warmer, more emotional atmosphere of the revivalistic era, the emphasis of urban congregations on culture and refinement, and the more recent tendency toward "experimental," "contemporary," or "groovy" expression. Several of these stages parallel developments throughout much of American Protestantism. At one time Disciples referred to their worship as "nonliturgical," meaning that they did not have a prescribed book of order. They have properly abandoned such language. At its most typical we can characterize their liturgy as Reformed in tone and catholic in shape. "Reformed in tone" means basically spare and restrained, a spirit nurtured by their

108

early roots in Scotland and Geneva. (Some early Disciples in northern Ohio even considered handshaking a demonstration of enthusiasm, almost too emotional to practice in church!) "Catholic in shape" means that the main service of worship each Lord's Day unites preaching and the eucharist, with a constant awareness also of the witness of baptism to the gospel.[42]

To speak first of baptism, in the days of large-scale conversion in America, Disciples grew with great rapidity, as did other churches emphasizing adult decision for membership. And the public immersion of the new converts became an important part of Disciples' witness to the gospel. From the meetinghouse they customarily repaired to a river or pond for the act of baptism, an occasion of reverent joy mingled with profound awe. When these people went down in winter to cut through the ice on a frozen stream in order to fulfil the ordinance of Christ, they experienced as profound a sense of the numinous as their hard-headed approach to religion permitted. Other services in kindlier climes moved them to idyllic descriptions of the beauty of the ordinance.[43]

In time, they installed baptistries in their churches. With rare exception in present buildings, the baptistry has been placed in the focal point at the rear of the chancel. Though commonly concealed by a dossal curtain when not in use, its prominence remains fixed in the consciousness of the worshipers. Many Disciples prize the memory of their own baptism, not only as the climactic step in their commitment to Christ, but also as a dramatic enactment of the apostolic faith in the death, burial, and resurrection of the Lord.

Disciples have softened the hard line they once followed on baptism. They widely practice open membership today. They have gladly affirmed with other churches the mutual recognition of members. They appear ready to accept alternative practices of baptism in a united church. Most assume that such a church should grant liberty for the ministration of immersion to a Christian who, not having received it, might request it. And they trust that the immersion of believers will continue as a dramatic witness to the faith of the church of the future.

As to the "breaking of bread," Disciples have made it a regular part of their weekly worship from the beginning. In frontier times, small congregations kept communion under the leadership of their ordained elders even when there was no preacher. To Christians familiar with other eucharistic traditions, the typical Disciples' liturgy of the table seems attenuated and lacking in liturgical character. The common pattern, however, includes the presentation of the offering, a communion hymn, a brief meditation making use of the words of institution, prayers of thanksgiving for bread and the cup, and distribution of the elements to the congregation. Individual cups are ordinarily used, and the worshipers commonly hold them in quiet meditation until all drink simultaneously. In recent years increasing numbers of Disciples have appropriated more of the traditional "catholic" action and shape of the eucharistic liturgy, generally keeping it, however, spare in tone and comparatively brief.[44]

Today a "professional" minister customarily presides at the table, almost universally assisted by local elders. In the absence of a minister, however, or on special occasions Disciples regard it as proper for elders to preside, and the old custom continues in many congregations. The COCU "Plan of Union" (1970) allowed for such an "eldership" by stipulating that elders may receive standing as local presbyters. Disciples cherish the ministry of elders. They see it as a significant contribution to the diversity of worship within the liberty of a united church.[45]

A New Emergent in Church Polity

The most difficult issue for any broadly conceived church union in America appears to be the issue of structure. The problem has not emerged as one of ecclesiology. When COCU released its 1970 "Plan of Union" for study by the member churches, relatively few theological objections were raised regarding bishops, conferences, and other institutional proposals. But the *operational* aspects of the suggested scheme aroused fears of encroachment on Christian liberty. Apparently much work remains to be done as Christians think their way through to a form of church which effectively expresses its oneness while at the same time safeguarding freedom. It seems appropriate therefore to report here on the experience of Disciples, since their "restructure" in 1968, with an emerging polity which preserves the essential freedom claimed by members and congregations throughout their history. At the same time it gives form to the corporate structure of the church in such a way as to provide for common action, the development of general policy, and the supervision of denominational life.

At the beginning of their history Disciples opted for congregational polity. Not only did it appeal to their emphasis, both practical and temperamental, on the local community of believers, but they long considered that it was mandated by

110

Scripture. While many of them no longer see it so clearly set forth in the New Testament, the freedom of the congregation to order its own life is universally accepted as a spiritual value of unquestionable theological validity. Yet the experience of a century and a half has led Disciples to conclude that congregations as such cannot do all the work of the church. For some decades this work was assigned to a variety of agencies, regional and general. But the conviction grew that it was, after all, the work of the church, not of secular corporations governed by individuals. O. L. Shelton said in 1955, "Disciples of Christ are struggling for a realization of the *church* among the churches, of a sense of the *universal church* among the local churches and the sense of plurality in *oneness* among the single congregations." In a new theological departure, Disciples shifted from speaking of the Christian *Churches* and began to speak of the Christian *Church* in a given region, or in the United States and Canada. They now conceived this church as a corporate institutional entity, not just an invisible fellowship or unstructured "brotherhood."[46]

In 1968 after an extended period of preparation, the last meeting of the old International Convention of Christian Churches (Disciples of Christ) adopted a proto-constitutional document called "A Provisional Design for the Christian Church (Disciples of Christ)." In an ecumenical context the Design set forth four components of the Christian Church—member, congregation, region, and general church—using the following words:

As a member of the whole body of Christ, every person who is or shall become a member of a recognized congregation of the Christian Church thereby holds membership in the Christian Church in his region and in the Christian Church in the United States and Canada.

These four components are held together in "free and voluntary relationships" by a covenant of mutual consent. Thus this new emergent in polity guarantees liberty in unity by basing itself on the two principles of voluntarism and mutual commitment. It empowers the church at large through the General Assembly to develop policies and procedures for the whole, which will be interpreted and administered by the regions, at the same time granting the right of any member or congregation to dissent "in love" from an action taken by the larger body.[47]

As Disciples discussed and moved toward this form of polity, many fears were expressed. A sizeable number of "independent" congregations formally requested removal of their names from the yearbook of the church, and influential Disciples who had been identified with the cooperative agencies through the years organized formal opposition (which soon quietly subsided). In time it became clear to nearly all that those who advocated restructure were genuinely committed to liberty, that the Provisional Design did in fact establish the general and regional manifestations of the church without threatening any rights previously enjoyed, and that personal and congregational freedoms were not hampered under the new development. Although adoption of the Design precipitated the withdrawal of the "independent" Christian Churches, within the new structure itself expressions of fear have virtually been forgotten. The provision of the Design for an appeal of grievances by persons, congregations, regions or boards who might feel themselves wronged has gone unused, for no one has felt the need to invoke it. The move into the new structure of relationships has involved a minimum of trauma.[48]

Under the Design, congregations elect voting representatives to biennial regional assemblies, which in turn elect the regional boards and establish regional policies. Congregations and regions elect voting representatives to the biennial General Assembly in which ordained ministers with certified standing also have the right to vote. The General Assembly is a large body commonly composed of five thousand voting representatives and an equal number of registered attendants with the privilege of the floor but not of the vote. This large assembly elects a General Board of some 200 members which meets annually and it in turn elects an Administrative Committee of about 40 members, which meets several times a year. This polity is certainly not traditional congregationalism, since it recognizes various "manifestations" of the church. It is not connectionalism in that the general and regional bodies exercise no legal authority over the congregations. So far as I know, it fits no other known polity. One might call it congregationalism-plus or consensus-connectionalism, or federal voluntarism, but none of these terms is likely to cause many hearts to leap up.

Three features of this polity should be of special pertinence to the church of the future as it seeks to provide both unity and liberty.

(1) *The Toleration of Anomaly.* In their regard for freedom Disciples have developed an ecclesiastical style which recognizes that not all people think alike nor do all accept a new idea at the same time. Such a situation offers a choice between diversity or coercion, and Disciples on principle opt for diver-

112

sity out of respect for liberty. They hold that what makes an action right is not just the action in itself but the choosing of that action in the conviction that it is right. They take decisions in the democratic way by majority vote. But the principle of free and voluntary relationships accords to the minority the right, not only of dissent from, but of non-participation in, a particular course of action. At the same time, the majority retains freedom to move ahead and implement the decision. Thus an action taken by the General Assembly becomes general policy for the Christian Church, to be carried out by the general office to the extent of its authority. It carries great moral weight with divisions and administrative units, regions, and congregations; their implementation of it, as it pertains to them and their work, depends on their own processes of decision-making.

Exercising responsibility in a context of Christian freedom, Disciples have evolved through the years a characteristic way of working. It involves initiative in proposing a new program or policy, the broadest possible discussion of the issues, movement toward a general consensus, formal adoption, initiation of the new policy by the consent of those involved, and concession that some will dissent or not participate. Such a procedure may offend those who love authority, speed, or neatness, but it works with reasonable effectiveness among a people committed both to mutuality and freedom. It allows for education (even moral pressure), for movement forward on the part of those who are ready, and for the gradual adoption of a new position as its value comes to be perceived.

In some matters Disciples practice a remarkable uniformity—in congregational observance of the eucharist every week, in the general tone of their worship, in congregational administrative structure, in the regions' constitution of their assemblies through voting representatives, to name a few. But no authoritative body ever legislated any of these procedures as a general requirement. The congregations and regions have adopted them of their own volition following widespread discussion and the example of others. Disciples believe in this process and it has worked better than might be expected. It takes freedom seriously. A member, minister, or congregation can get out of the Christian Church almost too easily, but it is virtually impossible to "throw out" any of these who want to stay.

Disciples commend to the church of the future the freedom which tolerates anomaly. One of the difficulties, I believe, plaguing the Consultation on Church Union was the emergence in the late 1960s of a kind of perfectionism which sought by legislation to guarantee an ideal state of affairs on every issue. It showed itself in a tendency to demand heroic decisions on all sorts of difficult and debatable matters as *prerequisite to* the establishment of a united church. The proposed parish in the 1970 "Plan of Union," for example, had much to commend it. It undertook to overcome congregational introversion, racism, and inequity of resources. But to many sincere Christians, the logic of the scheme was not compelling, much less its mandatory character. They simply were not able to transfer the loyalty they held toward their congregations to any such hypothetical entity, nor were they prepared to agree in advance to turn over their property to it. Disciples would say of any such proposal: Don't try to legislate perfection in advance. Don't make acceptance of the parish a condition of union. Rather set up the possibility of the new procedure. Commend it with all urgency. Discuss it widely. Initiate it wherever people show readiness for it. Leave the option open. Give congregations time to experiment with it and to grow into it. Union will be hard enough to achieve under any circumstance, without appearing to shut off familiar freedoms or requiring acceptance in advance of procedures no one has yet tried. Expect all who enter a united church to commit themselves anew to Christ, to his will for his church, to all who share its life with them, and to an orderly process of decision-making. Then let them grow in mutual understanding of what that commitment means. And don't be afraid of anomaly for a time. (If someone still wants to celebrate the Tridentine mass in Latin, why not?)

(2) *Distribution of Responsibility.* Although the polity of the Christian Church operates through congregational, regional, and general structures, it is not hierarchical. Rather each manifestation of the church takes decision and action in those areas for which it is responsible. This system of "free and responsible relationships" is much more similar to the federal structure of nation, state, and municipality than it is to a military or corporate chain of command. (Nation, state, and municipality are interrelated. The same person is citizen of all three. But each makes only the decision appropriate to its own sphere.) Although administration "from the top down" may maximize a certain kind of efficiency at the cost of freedom, Disciples believe that freedom for local and regional initiative makes for greater efficiency in those parts of the church and for greater health throughout.

Disciples would commend to the united church of the future a structure which keeps decision-making and implementation close to the people concerned. We need to learn to think horizontally rather than vertically in designing procedures for a united church; that is, to spread its resources of staff broadly at the base where they are available to and responsive to the local churches rather than piling them up as a great bureaucracy at the top or stacking them in a massive pyramid. In a united church with many members, the districts or dioceses can be geographically small and still numerically strong, close to the people, responsive to needs, expressive of freedom.[49]

(3) *Voluntarism as the Necessary Mode of Freedom.* Not long after the people of the United States had guaranteed by their Constitution civil and religious liberty for all, Disciples of Christ came on the scene. Sharing in the democratic ethos of the American people, they undertook a new experiment in the life of the church, committed both to unity and to freedom. The first article in the national Bill of Rights had ruled out all coercion by the state in matters of religion. Voluntarism was to be the rule. Embracing that principle in all seriousness, Disciples also excluded coercion from the internal life of the church and appealed to the New Testament for validation of the principle.

Both by temperament and conviction, Disciples applied the rule of voluntarism with consistency. Baptism and church membership were for those who freely responded of their own volition to the gospel of Jesus Christ. The discipline of the church, the vitality of its program, its financial support, all depend on the free response of its members. The policies of a congregation, its participation in the life of the larger church, its action regarding any duty which others see as clearly imcumbent upon all Christians depends entirely on its own responsiveness to the will of Christ and on its own decision.

While the "Provisional Design" balances the paragraph on rights with one on responsibilities, no institutional power anywhere along the line can say to a region, congregation, or member, "Do this, or else . . . ." Yet without instruments of coercion Disciples have developed a remarkably dynamic and integrated institutional life. This is not to say that they are more virtuous than others, that donors, elders, ministers, or denominational officials have not built up their little empires based on whatever accidental power they might manage to exert in a given situation. But any such effort to throw their weight around derived from original sin, not from their doctrine of the church.[50]

Disciples believe that any right action must spring from a moral decision if it is to have Christian significance and that "nothing can be moral that is not voluntary." Accordingly they have undertaken to build a church which relies on education, discussion, persuasion, and voluntary decision. They have the means to take responsible actions by which units of the church and members who are persuaded may move ahead, but they believe that those not so persuaded have the right to await their own good time. Consequently Disciples believe in "leaving the door open" to those who may arrive at a decision later than the majority, hesitating to exclude them or put them at disadvantage. Disciples commend to the church of the future the genius of this polity of consensus which relies on loyalty.[51]

Forward in Freedom

Two hundred years ago the people of the thirteen colonies launched a bold experiment in liberty. The idealism of that political venture became a shining vision for the colonists, for millions of immigrants who flocked to this land in hope of a better life, for their children, and for peoples in all parts of the world who dared to dream of freedom. It is still a revolutionary ideal.

In the second generation of the young republic a new religious movement arose, with a cardinal commitment to freedom. It grew and prospered in the open atmosphere of voluntarism which pervaded the new nation. Calling themselves Christians or Disciples of Christ, its members loved political liberty and made their contribution to its extension. They sought the emancipation of the human spirit through evangelism and education as they lived out the faith of the free. They determined to achieve liberty in the church, to break the chains holding it captive in sectarianism and preoccupation with non-essentials. Their experiment in liberty led them to test and then to reject certain means designed to assure freedom. But in loyalty to Christ and in love for his people they have persisted in working out the logic of their commitment. At the conclusion of his massive *Comprehensive History of the Disciples of Christ*,[52] the scholarly W. T. Moore, breaking into verse, hailed this people as ". . . a free and noble brotherhood."

Because the issues of freedom are universal and eternal, they reach far beyond the United States and the experience of one religious group. The struggle for political and economic liberation today challenges oppression in every part of the world. With the collapse of old cultures and the spread of pluralism, persons everywhere are faced with new choices in the effort to achieve personal freedom. Called amidst all this confusion and longing to make known a liberating gospel, the whole church faces issues of overwhelming importance regarding its own life: Will it be free to respond to Jesus Christ? Free for its mission of service and liberation in the world? Free to demonstrate a distinctive Christian ethos and lifestyle? Free to appropriate in all its parts the healing of ecumenical wholeness, to rejoice in a unity which encompasses diversity, to accept its oneness in Christ and to manifest that fulness of life in him to all the world?

To the church, as to all people everywhere who catch a vision of the liberty offered by Jesus Christ, comes one sure word: "If, therefore, the Son makes you free, you will be free indeed."[53]

NOTES

Preface

1. Van Meter Ames (ed.), *Beyond Theology: the Autobiography of Edward Scribner Ames* (Chicago: The University of Chicago Press, 1959):82. Frederick Sontag and John K. Roth treat the concern for freedom as one of the three distinctive marks of American theology in their work, *The American Religious Experience: The Roots, Trends, and Future of American Theology* (New York: Harper & Row Publishers, 1972).

2. "First Principles: Liberty" (editorial), *The Christian-Evangelist* 49 (April 25, 1912):580; *Cf.* 616; *ibid.,* 1912 (May 2, 1912):616; "The Disciples and Freedom," *ibid.,* 88 (October 11, 1950):987; "Disciples and Freedom," *ibid.,* 89 (November 28, 1951):1143.

3. In centering on the motifs of *restoration* and *unity,* historians of the movement have generally followed the line taken by W. T. Moore in his centennial history. His theological prologue, which falls just short of 100 pages, emphasizes "the Scripturalness of the Plea" and its "unsectarianism." Though liberty is implicit he does not develop it as a theme. William Thomas Moore, *A Comprehensive History of the Disciples of Christ: Being an Account of a Century's Effort to Restore Primitive Christianity in Faith, Doctrine and Life* (New York: Fleming H. Revell Company, 1909):73-96.

   W. E. Garrison has been the most influential historian of the movement. In "An Overview: the Main Stream of Disciple Thought," in A. T. DeGroot, *Disciple Thought: a History* (Fort Worth, Texas: Author, Texas Christian University, 1965):3, Garrison clearly states the prevailing formula of interpretation:

   There seems to be no superior substitute for the time-honored description of the thought and practice of the Disciples as centering upon two major objectives—the unity of Christians in one church and restoration of all that was designed to be permanent in primitive Christianity.

   References to freedom in the historians and commentators tend to be suggestive rather than systematic.

   Eva Jean Wrather, in "Alexander Campbell—Portrait of a Soul: A Quest for Freedom," *The Christian-Evangelist* 76 (Sept. 8, 1938):964, writes:

   With a consuming passion for liberty, both religious and political—which motivated his whole life from the day in his boyhood when his imagination was first stirred by stories of the French and American revolutions—Alexander Campbell joined a spirit of devout obedience to the will of God. "I call no man master upon the earth," he wrote; but he bowed unquestionably before any precept he conceived to be a commandment of the Christ. Hence, the theology he professed was a compound of liberty and authority, a union of vital elements in both Protestantism and Catholicism.

   Carter E. Boren, *Religion on the Texas Frontier* (San Antonio, Texas: The Naylor Company, 1968):340, writes:

   There was an abiding positive concern for the freedom of the Christian man. These Texans endeavored to maintain what, as Disciples of Christ, they believed to be the scriptural basis for a united church, and at the same time sought to carry on its operations by a democratic process which was at once in uniformity with three phases of their culture; namely, the Christian freedom that is found in the New Testament, the natural rights of man, and the democratic society of which they formed a part.

The latest major history of the movement—William E. Tucker and Lester G. McAllister, *Journey in Faith: A History of the Christian Church (Disciples of Christ)* (St. Louis, Missouri: The Bethany Press, 1975):21 observes, "Disciples, in short, prize freedom and are not of a mind to feel guilty about their diversity."

A few authors make *explicit mention of freedom* as a cardinal emphasis conjoined *with liberty and restoration,* but the theme of liberty has not received the systematic treatment throughout the life of the movement which historians have accorded the other two emphases. Among more specialized works, two studies of Alexander Campbell may be mentioned: James Egbert, *Alexander Campbell and Christian Liberty* (St. Louis: Christian Publishing Company, 1909) and D. Ray Lindley, *Apostle of Freedom* (St. Louis, Mo.: The Bethany Press, 1957). The latter, a critical analysis of Campbell's ecclesiology, reveals the affinities between his doctrine of the church and the American political context.

While the historians have not yet linked *liberty* with *unity* and *restoration* as determining and interrelated emphases, a few Disciples have done so. Some suggestive references may be noted.

John B. Cowden, in *Saint Paul on Christian Unity: An Exposition of the Epistle to the Ephesians* (New York: Fleming H. Revell Company, 1923), devotes a chapter to "Liberty and Unity." The interrelatedness of these two motifs with restoration is explicit in his mention of "the essentials of unity, with respect to which there is no liberty. Liberty has to do with the nonessentials" (p. 187). "There is no liberty to do or not do what the Spirit of the Lord requires" in the Scriptures; "yet within these requirements there is the largest freedom" (p. 193).

Edwin V. Hayden, "Can the Church Have Liberty, Unity, and Restoration?" *Christian Standard,* (May 20, 1950):315 said to the North American Christian Convention: "the church . . . can and must have liberty and unity *by* restoration."

James DeForest Murch entitled one of his books *The Free Church: A Treatise on Church Polity with Special Reference to Doctrine and Practice in Christian Churches and Churches of Christ* (Louisville, Ky.: Restoration Press, 1966). While the book gives some historical perspective, the author himself characterizes it as "a polemic" (p. 5). His history, *Christians Only: A History of the Restoration Movement* (Cincinnati, Ohio: Standard Publishing Company, 1962), centers on the restoration theme.

Henry K. Shaw, "The New Reformation and the Church Today" (Worship Bulletins, UCMS/CBP, W2 7/14/68) writes:

There seem to have been three principles emphasized in what was then called the 'new' Reformation. They were: (1) the authority of Scripture in matters of faith and order, (2) unity of all God's people, and (3) individual freedom.

From some notes which the late Walter W. Sikes loaned me, I put down five "dynamic principles" which he observed in the mind of Disciples:

1. *The motive of catholicity*
2. *A return to a primitive pattern of perfection*
3. *An authoritative biblical revelation*
4. *The appeal to rational inquiry and empirical experience in the search for truth*

5. *Democratic freedom—freedom of thought and a democratic polity.*

4. The interrelationship among restoration, freedom, and unity was discussed in my essay, "Formula in Flux: Reformation for the Disciples of Christ?" in Kyle Haselden and Martin E. Marty (eds.), *What's Ahead for the Churches? A Report from THE CHRISTIAN CENTURY* (New York: Sheed & Ward, 1964):112-122; reprinted in *The Christian Century,* 80 (September 25, 1963):1163-1166. The issue will receive further comment in Lecture 3.

5. David Edwin Harrell, Jr., *A Social History of the Disciples of Christ,* Vol. II, *The Social Sources of Division in the Disciples of Christ, 1865-1900* (Atlanta and Athens, Georgia: Publishing Systems, Inc., 1973): 350 and *passim. Cf.* the chapter on "Diversity" in Kenneth L. Teegarden, *We Call Ourselves Disciples* (St. Louis, Missouri: The Bethany Press, 1975):50-56. *Cf.* Winfred E. Garrison, *Heritage and Destiny: An American Religious Movement Looks Ahead* (St. Louis, Missouri: The Bethany Press, 1961): 124, 153. For the three major bodies into which the movement has divided, see my article, "Disciples of Christ," in *Encyclopaedia Britannica,* 15th ed., 1974.

6. Marion B. Brinson, H. G. Haney, and G. Edwin Osborn (eds.), *A Century with Christ: A Story of the Christian Church in Richmond* ([Richmond, Virginia:] Editorial Committee of the Disciples Centennial General Committee, 1932).

7. See "Society Official Cited by Transylvania: Forrest F. Reed Honored," *The Harbinger and Discipliana* 14 (May, 1954):5.

8. Alexander Campbell, *The Sacred Writings of the Apostles and Evangelists of Jesus Christ, Commonly Styled the New Testament,* Translated from the Original Greek by Doctors George Campbell, James MacKnight and Philip Doddridge, with Prefaces, Various Emendations, and An Appendix. 2nd Stereotyped Ed. (Cincinnati: Franklin & Rice, 1870). A. Campbell's preface is dated January 29, 1826. *Cf.* Cecil K. Thomas, *Alexander Campbell and His New Version* (St. Louis, Missouri: The Bethany Press, 1958).

9. See the memorial issue of *Discipliana* 35 (Spring, 1975) with a series of articles on J. Edward Moseley. Along with innumerable articles, he wrote *Disciples of Christ in Georgia* (St. Louis, Missouri: The Bethany Press, 1954) and *The Concern for Benevolence among Disciples of Christ* (St. Louis: National Benevolent Association of the Christian Churches, 1957), and edited *Evangelism—Commitment and Involvement: "God . . . Reconciling the World,"* The N. E. A. Lectures on Evangelism for 1964 (St. Louis: The Bethany Press, 1965).

10. Claude E. Spencer, *Theses Concerning the Disciples of Christ, the Churches of Christ, and the Christian Church* (Canton, Mo.: Disciples of Christ Historical Society, 1941); *Periodicals of the Disciples of Christ and Related Religious Groups* (Canton, Mo.: Disciples of Christ Historical Society, 1943); *An Author Catalog of Disciples of Christ and Related Religious Groups* (Canton, Mo.: Disciples of Christ Historical Society, 1946); "Poets, Hymn Writers, Fiction Writers and Story Tellers of the Disciples of Christ" (Charlestown, Ind.: mimeographed by Charles Willard, 1959). He initiated and directed the preparation of *The Christian-Evangelist Index, 1863-1958* (Published jointly—St. Louis, Mo. Christian Board of Publication and Nashville, Tennessee Disciples of Christ Historical Society, 1962) and *Christian Standard Index 1866-1966,* (Nashville, Tennessee: Disciples of Christ Historical Society, 1972).

11. Henry King Shaw, *Saga of a Village Church, 1877-1937: The Story of Religion in Medina and the Founding and Accomplishments of the Church of Christ, Medina, Ohio* (Medina, O.: Church of Christ, 1937); *Buckeye*

Disciples: A History of the Disciples of Christ in Ohio, A Centennial Publication of the Ohio Christian Missionary Society, 1852-1952 (St. Louis: Christian Board of Publication, 1952); Hoosier Disciples: A Comprehensive History of the Christian Churches (Disciples of Christ) in Indiana (St. Louis: the Bethany Press for the Association of the Christian Churches in Indiana, 1966). For the story of the cigar, see his letter, "I'll Try . . . 'Alexander Campbells,' " The Christian-Evangelist 75 (March 4, 1937):290.

12. David Brinkley, "A Treasure to Share," Saturday Review (June 26, 1976): 7; Norman Cousins, "Forgotten Revolution," ibid. (July 10, 1976):4.

Lecture 1, Spirit of a Free People: The Democratic Ethos of Disciples of Christ

1. Pauline Maier, "Coming to Terms with Samuel Adams," The American Historical Review 80 (Feb., 1976):14.
2. "Toasts to the Fourth," Indiana History Bulletin 41 (July, 1969):91-92.
3. For Alexander Campbell's pride in the national domain, see his 1847 "Baccalaureate Address to the Graduates of Bethany College," in his Popular Lectures and Addresses (Philadelphia: James Challen & Son, 1863):494.
4. R. Carlyle Buley, The Old Northwest: Pioneer Period, 1815-1840, 2 vols. (Bloomington: Indiana University Press, 1951), I, 122-123; II, 381-384, 580-597.
5. Speech in the U.S. House of Representatives, April 22, 1846. Quoted by Buley, op. cit., II, 328.
6. Vachel Lindsay, "The Statue of Old Andrew Jackson," Collected Poems, rev. ed. with illustrations by the author (New York: The Macmillan Company, 1913):92.
7. W. F. Dunaway, The Scotch-Irish of Colonial Pennsylvania (Chapel Hill: The University of North Carolina Press, 1944):49, 134, 174, 178.
8. Frederick A. Norwood, The Story of American Methodism: A History of the United Methodists and Their Relations (Nashville: Abingdon Press, 1974): 98-101, 124-129; Winfred Ernest Garrison and Alfred T. DeGroot, The Disciples of Christ: A History (St. Louis, Missouri: Christian Board of Publication, 1948):84-87. Hope Hull supported O'Kelly's motion, but stayed with the Methodist Episcopal Church; later he profoundly influenced the young Barton W. Stone; see Charles Crossfield Ware, Barton Warren Stone, Pathfinder of Christian Union: A Story of His Life and Times (St. Louis, Missouri: The Bethany Press, 1932):37-38. After Stone's move to Kentucky, Haggard also went West and persuaded the Springfield Presbytery to take the name Christian Church.
9. Sidney E. Ahlstrom, A Religious History of the American People (New Haven: Yale University Press, 1972):446; Garrison and DeGroot, op. cit., pp. 81, 88-89. The Herald of Gospel Liberty has been hailed as the first American religious newspaper; it was however preceded by another periodical, the Connecticut Evangelical Magazine, which appeared in 1800; see Richard C. Wolf, "The Middle Period," Religion in Life 22 (Winter, 1952-53): 82. I am grateful to President Emeritus Ross J. Griffeth, a descendant of Roger Williams, for suggestive comments, in a recent letter, on the significance of the Freewill Baptists.
10. Declaration and Address and Last Will and Testament of the Springfield Presbytery (1949 Centennial Edition. Indianapolis, Indiana: International Convention of Disciples of Christ, 1949):57; cf. Garrison and DeGroot, op. cit., pp. 109-116.

121

11. *Declaration and Address,* pp. 14-15. James Moffatt, *The Presbyterian Churches,* 2nd ed. (London: Methuen & Co., Ltd., 1928):78; John Prebble, *The Lion in the North: A Personal View of Scotland's History* (Harmondsworth, Middlesex, England: Penguin Books, 1971):242.

12. *Declaration and Address, op. cit.,* pp. 7-8.

13. Campbell, *Popular Lectures and Addresses,* pp. 174, 229; *cf.* pp. 33, 189-190, 483-484, 498-503.

14. *Ibid.,* p. 298.

15. *Ibid.,* pp. 181, 298, 367. For the influence of Locke, see Winfred Ernest Garrison, *Alexander Campbell's Theology: Its Sources and Historical Setting* (St. Louis: Christian Publishing Company, 1900):108. For "The New Revolution of July 4," see Robert Frederick West, *Alexander Campbell and Natural Religion* (New Haven:Yale University Press, 1948):3-6. See also Leroy Garrett, *Alexander Campbell and Thomas Jefferson: A Comparative Study of Two Old Virginians* (Dallas, Texas: Wilkinson Publishing Co., 1963).

16. Campbell, *Popular Lectures and Addresses,* pp. 262-270; *cf.* Garrison and DeGroot, *op. cit.,* pp. 199-200.

17. Campbell, *Popular Lectures and Addresses,* pp. 184, 309; Carey J. Gifford, "Whig and Jacksonian Politics, and Alexander Campbell: Some Spatio-Temporal Considerations" (Claremont, California: Claremont Graduate School and University Center, Unpublished paper, 1975):20; Ernest Lee Tuveson, *Redeemer Nation: The Idea of America's Millennial Role* (Chicago: The University of Chicago Press, 1968):217. For a critique of the common tendency to commend one's denomination because of its affinity with the American character and institutions, see Will Herberg, "Protestantism in a Post-Protestant America," *Christianity and Crisis* 32 (Feb. 5, 1962): 3-7. On Campbell and civil religion, see Richard T. Hughes, "Alexander Campbell: A Classic Bicentennial Figure," *Discipliana* 36 Fall, 1976): 27-29; *cf.* my paper, "Peril to Christianity or Opportunity for Ecumenism? A Consideration of American Civil Religion," *Encounter* 37 (Summer, 1976): 245-258.

18. Campbell, *op. cit.,* p. 227; *cf.* pp. 239, 244, 269; Marvin D. Williams, Jr., "It Has Been Said . . . Alexander Campbell and Congress," *Discipliana* 25 (March, 1965): 10-11, 15; Arthur A. Azlein, "Campbell in the Capital," *The Disciple* 3 (April 4, 1976): 37-38.

19. For the land, see Campbell, *op. cit.,* pp. 249, 105. For national destiny, *ibid.,* p. 497; *cf.* Perry E. Gresham, "Alexander Campbell and the American Dream," *The Disciple* 2 (Aug. 3, 1975):6-7; *cf.* Gresham, "Alexander Campbell, Patriot" *Christian Standard* 110 (Oct. 5, 1975): 19-20. For the Protestant heritage, Campbell, *op. cit.,* pp. 167-179, 453. For the millennium, *ibid.,* pp. 594-599.

20. Campbell, *op cit.,* p. 352. *cf.* David Edwin Harrell, Jr., *A Social History of the Disciples of Christ:* Vol. I, *Quest for a Christian America: The Disciples of Christ and American Society to 1866* (Nashville, Tennessee: The Disciples of Christ Historical Society, 1966):52-53, 62-63, 111; *cf.* Harold L. Lunger, *The Political Ethics of Alexander Campbell* (St. Louis, Missouri: The Bethany Press, 1954):197; *cf.* William E. Tucker and Lester G. McAllister, *Journey in Faith: A History of the Christian Church (Disciples of Christ)* (Saint Louis, Missouri: The Bethany Press, 1975):193.

21. Campbell, *op, cit.,* p. 535. Henry K. Shaw has stated Campbell's views on slavery quite neatly: "As he interpreted scripture, he thought slavery was acceptable in God's sight. From the political standpoint, he upheld the institution because it was sanctioned by law. Economically and socially, he was against slavery and thought it a curse to the country." See

Shaw, *Buckeye Disciples,* p. 140; *cf.* pp. 141-146, 181-183, 188, 193-196, 199-202; *cf.* Harrell, *op. cit.,* I, 100-107, 111; Lunger, *op. cit.,* pp. 193-232.

22. Elmira J. Dickinson (ed.), *A History of Eureka College, with Biographical Sketches and Reminiscences* (St. Louis: Christian Publishing Company, 1894); J. Edward Moseley, "Vantage Ground of Freedom: The Consequences of a Pioneer Disciple's Liberation of Slaves," *World Call* 37 (Feb., 1955): 16-17; J. Edward Moseley, *Disciples of Christ in Georgia* (St. Louis, Missouri: The Bethany Press, 1954):183-184.

23. David Edwin Harrell, Jr., "The Sectional Origins of the Churches of Christ," *The Journal of Southern History* 30 (Aug., 1964): 261-277.

24. For Disciples and the Ku Klux Klan, see Tucker and McAllister, *op. cit.,* pp. 356-358; Frank Elon Davison, *Thru The Rear-View Mirror* (St. Louis: The Bethany Press, 1955):75-79. My personal diary for April 14, 1971 has an extended entry recounting a conversation with a Disciple who had learned of active participation in the Klan by a member of his family and other ministers on the Pacific coast. For the Christian Crusade, see James Morris, *The Preachers,* illustrations by Tom Huffman (New York: St. Martin's Press, 1973):257-314.

25. William Baxter, *Life of Elder Walter Scott,* The Walter Scott Centennial Edition, Abridged by B. A. Abbott (St. Louis, Missouri: The Bethany Press, 1926):16-18, 28-29, 203-210; Dwight E. Stevenson, *Walter Scott, Voice of the Golden Oracle: A Biography* (St. Louis, Missouri: Christian Board of Publication, 1946):218; Eva Jean Wrather, " 'My Most Cordial and Indefatigable Fellow Laborer': Alexander Campbell Looks at Walter Scott, 1821-1861," *The Christian-Evangelist* 84 (Oct. 23, 1946): 1044-1045; Henry K. Shaw, "Eloquence in Frontier Evangelism," *Front Rank* 55 (October 27, 1946): 1-2, 12.

26. Walter Scott, *The Messiahship, or Great Demonstration, written for the Union of Christians, on Christian Principles, as Plead for in the Current Reformation* ([Cincinnati: H. S. Bosworth, 1859] facsimile ed., Kansas City, Mo.: Old Paths Book Club, n.d.), Chap. LIII, "New Government and New Society: United States Government," pp. 321, 332, 334.

27. Campbell on Johnson, *Millennial Harbinger,* 1838, p. 192; quoted by Ware, *op. cit.,* p. 294. Hoke S. Dickinson supplied me with the Rogers inscription.

28. Campbell, *Popular Lectures and Addresses,* p. 365; Harrell, *A Social History of the Disciples of Christ,* I, pp. 53-58. For the "nonpolitical view of politics," see Oliver Read Whitley, *Trumpet Call of Reformation* (St. Louis, Missouri: The Bethany Press, 1959):219-222.

29. J. Edward Moseley, "Women of Central," An Address Delivered to the Christian Women's Fellowship of Central Christian Church, Indianapolis, Indiana, on Thursday, March 10, 1966 (mimeographed); Henry K. Shaw, "Carry Nation," *Front Rank* 56 (September 7, 1947):2, 14.

30. For nineteenth-century Disciples in politics, see Murch, *Christians Only,* pp. 198-199.

31. For J. S. Black, see Homer Carey Hockett, *The Constitutional History of the United States, 1826-1876: A More Perfect Union* (New York: The Macmillan Company, 1939):262-267; William N. Brigance, *A History and Criticism of American Public Address,* 2 vols. (New York: Russell and Russell, 1943), Vol. I; Jeremiah S. Black, *Essays and Speeches of,* with a biographical sketch by Chauncey Black (New York: D. Appleton & Co., 1885).

32. For Thomas and Sally Lincoln, see Frederick D. Kershner, "Abraham Lincoln and the Disciples," *Shane Quarterly* 4 (April, 1943): 61-71; *cf.* Kershner, "As I Think on These Things: Valuable Lincoln Data Found," *The Christian-Evangelist* 80 (April 30, 1942): 478-479. For the O'Kane legend, see Murch, *Christians Only,* p. 155; *cf.* Harley Patterson, "Abra-

Lincoln's statement about the church, see Edgar DeWitt Jones, *Lincoln and the Preachers,* Intro. by William H. Townsend (New York: Harper & Brothers Publishers, 1948):141; *cf.* Ames, *Beyond Theology,* pp. 166-167.

33. Willis R. Jones, " 'The Abiding Lincoln' and 'The Abiding Jones,' " *The Disciple* (Feb. 15, 1976): 12-14; Louis A. Warren, *Lincoln's Youth, Indiana Years: Seven to Twenty-One, 1816-1830* (Indianapolis: Indiana Historical Society, 1959); *cf.* Jim McKinney, "Louis Warren: Man of Lincoln," *The Christian-Evangelist* 95 (July 8, 1957): 867-869, 876.

34. Garfield, "On the Constitutional Amendment to Abolish Slavery," in the House of Representatives, January 13, 1865; in B. A. Hinsdale, *The Republican Text-Book for the Campaign of 1880. A Full History of General James A. Garfield's Public Life, with Other Political Information* (New York: D. Appleton and Company, 1880):98. Garfield, "Speech Nominating Sherman for President," June 5, 1880, in William Jennings Bryan and Francis W. Halsey (eds.) *The World's Famous Orations,* 10 vols. (New York: Funk and Wagnalls Company, 1906), X, p. 103. For Garfield's patriotism and some personal expressions of religion, see James A. Garfield, *The Wild Life of the Army: Civil War Letters of James A. Garfield,* ed. with an intro. by Frederick D. Williams (Lansing: Michigan State University Press, 1964):56-66, 89-90, 210. *cf.* W. W. Wasson, *James A. Garfield: His Religion and Education, A Study in the Religious and Educational Thought and Activity of an American Statesman* (Nashville: Tennessee Book Company, 1952):126-141; Donald Charles Lacy, "Garfield's Inaugural Address," *Discipliana* 35 (Winter, 1975): 39-40.

35. Clarke Newlon, *L. B. J.: The Man from Johnson City* (New York: Dodd, Mead & Company, 1964):114; *cf.* pp-32-33; Lyndon B. Johnson, *Public Papers of the Presidents of the United States: Containing the Public Messages, Speeches, and Statements of the President, 1963-1964* (In Two Books), Book I—November 22, 1963 to June 30, 1964 (Washington: United States Government Printing Office, 1965), 506-507; Doris Kearns, *Lyndon Johnson and the American Dream* (New York: Harper & Row, Publishers, 1976):229; George R. Davis, "L. B. J.: A President's Pastor Remembers a Layman Whose Faith Stayed Strong," *The Disciple* 4 (Jan. 2, 1977):7.

36. Mary L. Hinsdale (ed.), *Garfield-Hinsdale Letters: Correspondence between James Abram Garfield and Burke Aaron Hinsdale* (Ann Arbor: University of Michigan Press, 1949):361. See also pp. 366, 374, 381, 405-417.

37. B. A. Hinsdale, *The American Government, National and State,* 2d rev. ed. (Chicago: Werner School Book Company, 1900):422.

38. Harold E. Fey, "Ecumenists of Our Times: Charles Clayton Morrison," *Mid-stream* 15 (July, 1976): 263-270; Harold E. Fey and Margaret Frakes (eds.), *The Christian Century Reader: Representative Articles, Editorials, and Poems Selected from More than Fifty Years of The Christian Century* (New York: Association Press, 1962), *passim;* Charles Clayton Morrison, *The Outlawry of War: A Constructive Policy for World Peace.* Foreword by John Dewey (Chicago: Willett, Clark & Colby, 1927); Charles Clayton Morrison, *Can Protestantism Win America?* (New York: Harper & Brothers, 1948).

39. For reflections on Protestantism and human freedom, see Winfred Ernest Garrison, *A Protestant Manifesto* (Nashville: Abingdon-Cokesbury Press, 1952):198-200; See also W. E. Garrison, *The Quest and Character of a United Church* (Nashville: Abingdon Press, 1957).

40. Harold E. Fey, "A Protestant View," in Dallin H. Oakes (ed.), *The Wall beween Church and State* (Chicago: University of Chicago Press, 1963); Harold E. Fey, *With Sovereign Reverence: The First 25 Years of Americans*

United (Silver Springs, Md.; Roger Williams Press, 1974); Harold E. Fey and D'Arcy McNickle, *Indians and Other Americans* (New York: Harper & Brothers Publishers, 1959; rev. ed., 1970). See also Fey's series of articles, "Can Catholicism Win America?" in *The Christian Century* 61 (1944): 1378-1380, 1409-1411, 1442-1444, 1476-1479, 1498-1500; 62 (1945), 13-15, 44-47, 74-76.

41. M. Searle Bates, *Religious Liberty: An Inquiry* (New York: Harper & Brothers Publishers, 1945):570-582; Harold E. Fey (ed.), *The Ecumenical Advance: A History of the Ecumenical Movement, Vol. 2,* Published on Behalf of the Committee on Ecumenical History, Geneva (Philadelphia: The Westminster Press, 1970):270-272; "Indian Assembly Votes for Religious Liberty," *The Christian Century* 66 (1947):612; P. Oomman Philip, "India Assembly Defines Rights," *ibid.,* 718-719; "A Survey of the Year 1948," *International Review of Missions* 38 (1949):29; "A Survey of the Year 1949," *ibid.,* 39 (1950):20; Wynn C. Fairfield, "Religious Liberty," Foreign Missions Conference of North America, 1950: Report of the Fifty-Seventh Annual Meeting (New York: National Council of the Churches of Christ in the U.S.A.):82. "Carried by yak," Searle Bates, correspondence with Lillian Moir, Feb. 9, 1977.

42. Walter D. MacClintock, "Religious Values of the Fine Arts," in Herbert L. Willett, Orvis F. Jordan, and Charles M. Sharpe (eds.), *Progress: Anniversary Volume of the Campbell Institute on the Completion of Twenty Years of History* (Chicago: Published for the Campbell Institute by the Christian Century Press, 1917):310-312. Claude E. Spencer lists some hundreds of names in "Poets, Hymn Writers, Fiction Writers and Story Tellers of the Disciples of Christ," 1959. Mention must be made here of the widely circulated compilations by Cynthia Pearl Maus, *Christ and the Fine Arts,* 1938; *The World's Great Madonnas,* 1947; *The Old Testament and the Fine Arts,* 1954; *The Church and the Fine Arts,* 1960—all published by Harper and Brothers.

43. Shaw, *Buckeye Disciples,* p. 244; Henry K. Shaw, "The 'Spirit of '76' and the Disciples of Christ," *Front Rank* 57 (July 4, 1948):6-7; William S. Murphy, "Revolutionary Painting: Tipsy Drummer Likely Model for 'Spirit of '76,' " Los Angeles *Times,* (April 27, 1976). Alexander Phimister Proctor, *Sculptor in Buckskin: An Autobiography,* ed. by Hester Elizabeth Proctor (Norman: University of Oklahoma Press, 1971):84-85.

44. Eva Jean Wrather, *History in Stone and Stained Glass for the Thomas W. Phillips Memorial* (Nashville, Tennessee: Disciples of Christ Historical Society, 1958), *passim; Symbolism in Stone on the Thomas W. Phillips Memorial* (Nashville, Tennessee: Disciples of Christ Historical Society, 1957).

45. E. L. Powell, *Savonarola, or The Reformation of a City, with Other Addresses on Civic Righteousness* (Louisville: Sheltman & Company, 1903): 95-96.

46. From *Sermons for Special Days* [p. 118] by Frederick D. Kershner. Copyright © 1922 George H. Doran Company. Reprinted by permission of Doubleday & Co., Inc.

47. Charles Reign Scoville, "The Purpose of the Ages," in the H. H. Peters, *Charles Reign Scoville: The Man and His Message* (St. Louis, Missouri: Bethany Press, 1924):251-252.

48. Edgar DeWitt Jones, *Lords of Speech: Portraits of Fifteen American Orators* (Chicago: Willett, Clark & Company, 1937). His sermon, "The American Dream" appears in his collection, *A Man Stood up to Preach, and Fifteen Other Sermons* (St. Louis, Missouri: The Bethany Press, 1943); the passage quoted is on page 223. For "The Greatening of Abraham Lincoln,"

see his collection, *Sermons I Love to Preach* (New York: Harper & Brothers, Publishers, 1953):136-146.

49. Charles S. Medbury, "My Creed," *The Christian-Evangelist* 95 (July 1, 1957):7 [843]. Passages on freedom and democracy by the preachers could be continued indefinitely. See also Herman Norton, *Rebel Religion: The Story of the Confederate Chaplains* (St. Louis, Missouri: The Bethany Press, 1961):76-80 (not specifically on Disciples); W. Earl Waldrop, *What Makes America Great* (St. Louis, Missouri: The Bethany Press, 1957).

50. William L. Stidger, *Men of the Great Redemption* (Nashville, Tennessee: Cokesbury Press, 1931):66-72; Marcellus R. Ely, "Edwin Markham Speaks in West, *The Christian-Evangelist* 70 (December 7, 1933):1581. Edwin Markham, "The Man with the Hoe," rev. version, copyright 1920, in Louis Untermeyer (ed.), *Modern American Poetry, Modern British Poetry: A Critical Anthology,* combined edition (New York: Harcourt, Brace and Company, 1936):109-110. For Millet's fatalism as to exploitation the authority is Yale Art Historian Robert Herbert, cited by Robert Hughes, "A Great Lost Painter," *Time* (Feb. 23, 1976):60.

51. Lindsay, "The Proud Farmer," and "In Praise of Johnny Appleseed," *Collected Poems,* pp. 71-72, 88-89.

52. Thomas Curtis Clark, "The Faith of Christ's Freemen," in Thomas Curtis Clark and Hazel Davis Clark (comp. and eds.), *Christ in Poetry: An Anthology* (New York: Association Press, 1952):247.

53. Lindsay, "Alexander Campbell," Collected Poems, p. 355-358. For American dependence on the vocabulary of religion, see Henry F. May, "The Recovery of American Religious History," *American Historical Review* 70 (Oct., 1964):79-92. For additional comments on the theme of this lecture, see my essay, "Dogmatically Absolute, Historically Relative: Conditioned Emphases in the History of Disciples of Christ," in W. B. Blakemore (gen. ed.), *The Renewal of Church: The Panel Reports,* 3 vols. (St. Louis, Missouri: The Bethany Press, 1963), I, "The Democratic Spirit"; 270-273, "The Sense of Destiny," 273-275.

Lecture 2, Liberating the Human Spirit: Some Personal Dimensions of Freedom

1. For comments of Stow Persons and Sidney E. Mead on the importance of attention to motivation in religious history, see Jerald C. Brauer (gen. ed.), *Essays in Divinity,* Vol. V, *Reinterpretation in American Church History* (Chicago: The University of Chicago Press, 1968): 185.

2. Baxter, *Life of Elder Walter Scott* (ed. Abbott): 17-18.

3. Hetty D'Spain's sons, Addison and Randolph Clark, founded Add-Ran Christian College, which continues in Texas Christian University. Boren, *Religion on the Texas Frontier,* p. 12; Garrison and DeGroot, *The Disciples of Christ: A History,* pp. 318-319. On Crockett, see Michael J. Arlen, "The Air: Bloodmarks on the Sylvan Glade," *The New Yorker,* Oct. 13, 1975, p. 148.

4. His conversion to Rome occurred within a few months of John Henry Newman's. Peter H. Burnett, *The Path which Led a Protestant Lawyer to the Catholic Church* (New York: Benziger Brothers, 1866): v-viii. *Cf.* C. F. Swander, *Making Disciples in Oregon* (Portland: Author, 1928): 24; E. B. Ware, *History of the Disciples of Christ in California* (Healdsburg, California: F. W. Cooke, 1916): 13-14.

5. Garrison and DeGroot, *op. cit.,* p. 476. In the minute books of the Hopkinsville church I read in 1939 the entry on the action taken regarding Alexander Cross.

6. Quidnunc, "Just Among Disciples: A Campbell Circus Clown," 81 *The Christian-Evangelist* (January 27, 1943):112.

7. Nearly forty years ago I read an account of the incident, but I cannot now discover the source. For Clark as a Disciple, see Andrew Wilson, "Some Personal Recollections of Champ Clark," 58 *The Christian-Evangelist* (March 24, 1921):333.

8. Garrison and DeGroot, *The Disciples of Christ: A History,* p. 366; John T. Brown, *Churches of Christ: A Historical, Biographical, and Pictorial History of Churches of Christ in the United States, Australasia, England and Canada* (Louisville, Kentucky: John P. Morton and Company, 1904): 169.

9. For Maclachlan, see *The Christian* (Kansas City, Missouri), 1929:486, 495, 588. I am grateful to Professor Samuel C. Pearson, Jr. of Southern Illinois University at Edwardsville for these references; Edward Scribner Ames, *Beyond Theology: The Autobiography of Edward Scribner Ames* (Chicago: University of Chicago Press, 1959) pp. 159-160; Brinson, Haney, and G. Edwin Osborn, *A Century with Christ: A Story of the Christian Church in Richmond* (Richmond, Virginia: Editorial Committee of the Disciples Centennial General Committee, 1932): 99-105. For Brite, see Colby D. Hall, *History of Texas Christian University: A College of the Cattle Frontier* (Fort Worth: Texas Christian University Press, 1947) *passim.* For "Boggess' Ride." see *The Christian-Evangelist* 37 (November 8, 1900):1419.

10. Winfred Ernest Garrison, *Wheeling through Europe* (St. Louis: Christian Publishing Company, 1900). For Hoven, see Ross J. Griffeth, *Crusaders for Christ: A History of Northwest Christian College, 1895-1971* (Eugene, Oregon: Northwest Christian College, 1971): 40. For the Watkinses, see Keith Watkins, "The Watkins-Kilgore Cross Country Bicycle Trip, June 24 through July 29, 1976" (azographed).

11. Vachel Lindsay, "Kansas," *Collected Poems,* pp. 150-152; See also Edgar Lee Masters, *Vachel Lindsay: A Poet in America* (New York: Charles Scribner's Sons, 1935): 226-249. On July 12, 1976, Henry K. Shaw wrote me: "Who among us achieved the most freedom in his lifetime? My nomination would be Vachel Lindsay. When he gave up his life insurance, bank account, and worldly attachments (including paying taxes) and went on the road reciting poetry for bread, he became a free man. Too bad he had to commit suicide or my point would be much better!"

12. Edgar DeWitt Jones, *American Preachers of To-Day: Intimate Appraisals of Thirty-Two Leaders* (Indianapolis: the Bobbs-Merrill Company, 1933): 205-206.

13. Her attendance at Christian Churches is a matter of oral tradition. My grandfather, W. A. Lanterman, often told of the Sunday she visited Hillman Street Church in Youngstown, Ohio and was welcomed with excessive cordiality by a straight-laced elder, much to the merriment of some of the deacons who knew the identity of the visitor.

14. Another bit of oral tradition. O. L. Shelton told me more than once about taking Dr. Dye to see the statue.

15. Dwight E. Stevenson, "Writing in the Dark," *The Christian* 108 (Dec. 27, 1970):1636-1638.

16. Los Angeles *Times,* April 16, 1976.

17. See John Wooden (as told to Jack Tobin), *They Call Me Coach* (Waco, Texas: Word Books, Publisher, 1973), *passim.*

18. "Books Briefly Noted," review of *Growing (Up) at Thirty-Seven,* by Jerry Rubin, *The New Yorker* (March 15, 1976):140.

19. W. Barnett Blakemore, Jr., " 'Jesus Is the Christ': Walter Scott's Theology," *The Christian-Evangelist* 84 (October 23, 1946):1056-1059. For the four great evangelists of the Disciples, see H. H. Peters, *Charles Reign Scoville; The Man and His Message,* pp. 19-21.

20. John Augustus Williams, *Life of Elder John Smith. With Some Account of the Rise and Progress of the Current Reformation* (St. Louis, Missouri: Christian Board of Publication, 1870): 56-69, 147.

127

21. Baxter, *Life of Elder Walter Scott*, p. 47; Garrison and DeGroot, *The Disciples of Christ: A History*, pp. 182-191. E. V. Zollars, *The Commission Executed, or A Study of the New Testament Conversions and Other Evangelistic Topics* (Cincinnati, Ohio: The Standard Publishing Company, 1912):54-55, 62, 97, 150-172, 286. For Rauschenberg, see "The Most Living Artist," *Time* (Nov. 29, 1976):54, 60.
22. *Declaration and Address and The Last Will and Testament of the Springfield Presbytery*, pp. 17, 57; Zollars, *The Commission Executed*, p. 226.
23. Consider the eloquent passage in Campbell, *Popular Lectures and Addresses*, pp. 504-505, with its confidence in Bishop Ussher's chronology and in Satan's rebellion as a datable event in world history. See p. 533.
24. For analogy between biblical doctrine and mathematics, see Campbell, *Popular Lectures and Addresses*, p. 596. "One may believe a proposition intellectually," Zollars, *The Commission Executed*, pp. 11-12. For the "simplicity that is in Christ," using the text of the King James Version, see John S. Sweeney, *Sweeney's Sermons*, (Nashville: Gospel Advocate Publishing Company, 1892). For "The Creed That Needs No Revision," see Zollars, *The Great Salvation* (Cincinnati: The Standard Publishing Company, 1895):240-264.
25. For the mentality of the movement, see Blakemore, *The Renewal of Church: The Panel Reports*, especially Dean Blakemore's "Reasonable, Empiric, Pragmatic: The Mind of Disciples of Christ," I, 161-183; and Ralph G. Wilburn's "Disciple Thought in Protestant Perspective: An Interpretation," II, 305-335. See also George G. Beazley, Jr., "Disciples, Episcopalians, and the Consultation on Church Union," *Mid-Stream* 6 (Winter, 1967):29-49, and "A Look at the Disciples for European Baptists," *ibid.*, 50-66.
26. Campbell: "Parents and school-masters . . . can do more than all the ministers, priests, and lawgivers in the world," *Millennial Harbinger* (1841):480. Campbell on debate, quoted by Robert Frederick West, *Alexander Campbell and Natural Religion* (New Haven: Yale University Press):67, n.3. For emancipation from ignorance, see Zollars *The Commission Executed*, pp. 41, 271-276.
27. Campbell, *Popular Lectures and Addresses*, p. 210; *Cf.* J. V. Coombs, *Religious Delusions: Studies of the False Faiths of Today* (Cincinnati: The Standard Publishing Company, 1904), *passim*. Deliverance from superstition was a favorite theme of F. H. Marshall of Phillips University (class notes March 21, 1939).
28. Campbell, *Popular Lectures and Addresses*, p. 397. E. R. Moon, *I Saw Congo* (Indianapolis: The United Christian Missionary Society, 1952):135.
29. Campbell, *Popular Lectures and Addresses*, p. 327; *Cf.* A. Campbell, *The Christian System in Reference to the Union of Christians and Restoration of Primitive Christianity as Plead by the Current Reformation*, 2nd. ed. ([Bethany, Virginia, 1839] St. Louis, Missouri: Christian Board of Publication, facsimile ed., n.d.):27-37; Royal Humbert (ed.), *A Compend of Alexander Campbell's Theology*, with commentary in the form of critical and historical footnotes (St. Louis, Missouri: The Bethany Press, 1961): 216-231. Frank N. Gardner, "Man and Salvation: Characteristic Ideas among Disciples of Christ," in Blakemore, *The Renewal of Church: The Panel Reports*, I, 135-157.
30. Zollars, *The Commission Executed*, p. 279; See also pp. 148, 187. Frank Hamilton Marshall, class lecture at Phillips University, noted by author, March 21, 1939. For the "truth of the gospel" as offering deliverance from sin, selfishness, and the "doctrines of men," see J. A. Seaton, "What is Expected of a Preacher?" in G. L. Brokaw (ed.), *Doctrine and Life, by Iowa Writers* (Des Moines, Iowa: Christian Index Publishing Co., 1898):55.

31. G. Edwin Osborn, "Making the Lame Walk," April 1, 1962, sermon type-script in archives of Disciples of Christ Historical Society, Nashville. For other narratives of conversion, see R. Frederick West, *God's Gambler* (Englewood Cliffs, New Jersey: Prentice-Hall, Inc., 1964); Norma Zimmer, *Norma* (Wheaton, Illinois: Tyndale House Publishers, Inc., 1976): 81-93; The latter tells of the preaching of J. Warren Hastings. For reflections on the power of the gospel. Zollars, *The Commission Executed,* pp. 38, 56-62, 156; "How Much Freedom Can You Stand?" *The European Evangelist* 19 "Freedom in Christ," *Blue and White* 48 (July-Aug., 1976):1-2.

32. E. L. Powell, *The Victory of Faith: Sermons and Addresses* (St. Louis: Christian Publishing Company, 1905):61-62; *Cf.* Zollars, *The Commission Executed,* p. 266; Edgar DeWitt Jones, *Sermons I Love to Preach:* "The Matterhorn of the Holy Scriptures" (pp. 25-35), "On Losing and Finding God" (pp. 36-44), "The Farther Shore" (pp. 69-80).

33. For editors, see David Edwin Harrell, Jr., *A Social History of the Disciples of Christ,* Vol. II, *The Social Sources of Division in the Disciples of Christ, 1865-1900* (Atlanta and Athens, Georgia: Publishing Systems, Inc., 1973): 115ff. For the impact of the world mission on movements for freedom, see Charles W. Forman, *The Nation and the Kingdom: Christian Mission in the New Nations* (New York: Friendship Press, 1964):20-29; *Cf.* Ames, *Beyond Theology,* p. 101.

34. H. D. C. Maclachlan, "The New Ideal" and "Evangelical Implications of the Social Task of the Church" in *Progress* (eds.) Willet, Jordan, and Sharpe, (Chicago: Christian Century Press, 1917):175-176, 186-188. "Your land shall shake," James Earl Ladd, *"As Much As In Me Is . . ." and Other Sermons* (Portland, Oregon: Beattie and Company, 1951):124. J. Irwin Miller, "How Free is Free?" (Indianapolis: Indiana Civil Rights Commission, 1965).

35. Ronald Osborn, "For God's Sake—and for Man's!—A Glimpse of Cleo W. Blackburn, Pioneer in Fundamental Education," *The Christian-Evangelist* 91 (1953):158-160; Rosa Page Welch, "People around the World are the Same," *Ibid.,* pp. 256-258; "Rosa Page Welch Returning from World Tour Describes Interest in U.S.A. Race Relations," *Ibid.,* p. 456; *Cf. Social Action News-Letter,* March, 1953, p. 4; *Cf.* F. E. Davison, *The Scroll,* September, 1951, p. 25. For Norman Ellington, see Virginia Stuhr, "Change: Mothers Cross the Barriers of Race and Status and Learn How to Use Their Freedom to Correct Society's Injustice," *The Disciple* (June 6, 1976): 38-39.

36. Based on notes taken by author during Kershner's address, June 3, 1952.

37. Daniel Cobb, "Mr. Nixon and the Court," *The Christian Century* 86 (Oct. 1, 1969):1245-1247; See also William Daniel Cobb, "Morality-in-the-Making: a New Look at Some Old Foundations," *Ibid.* 92 (Jan. 1-8, 1975):8-12. William R. Barr, "The Struggle for Freedom in America: A Theological Critique," *Encounter* 37 (Summer, 1976):243-244. Lindsay, "Alexander Campbell," *Collected Poems,* p. 355-358. Clark Williamson, *God is Never Absent* (St. Louis, Mo.: Bethany Press, 1977):47.

38. Linnie Marsh Wolfe, *Son of the Wilderness: A life of John Muir* (New York: Alfred A. Knopf, 1945), pp. 82ff., 108ff. For a family's long and earnest involvement in the Christian Church, ended in the twentieth century because the younger generations could not abide the old rigidities, see William Maxwell, *Ancestors* (New York: Alfred A. Knopf, 1971), *passim.* *Cf.* "Joseph Fort Newton and the Disciples," *Discipliana* (July, 1946):19, 23. F. E. Davison, *I Would Do It Again: Sharing Experiences in the Christian Ministry* (St. Louis, Missouri: The Bethany Press, 1948). The "saints of the brotherhood" comes from personal memory.

39. G. Edwin Osborn, "The Disciplined Art of Arriving," Sermon #114, June

25, 1961, typescript in DCHS archives.

40. Peter Ainslie, *My Brother and I: A Brief Manual of the Principles that Make for a Wider Brotherhood with All Mankind* (New York: Fleming H. Revell Company, 1911):61.

41. Russell Chandler, "Californian to Head Baptist Churches. Group's Sixth Woman President," Los Angeles *Times* (June 25, 1977). Jean Woolfolk served as moderator of the General Assembly in San Antonio, Texas in 1975, and Walter Bingham in Cincinnati in 1973, each having been elected at the assembly two years before presiding. Mossie Allman Wyker presided over the Chicago assembly of the International Convention in 1952, but did so in her capacity as first vice president, the president being unable to attend. *Cf.* chap III, n.16. Because the Christian Woman's Board of Missions was one of the agencies which came together to form the United Christian Missionary Society, it secured an agreement that half the board members of the new body should be women, a provision continued by the Division of Homeland Ministries and the Division of Overseas Ministries, but by no other units of the restructured church.

42. "The Disciples and Liberty" (editorial), *The Christian-Evangelist,* (January 3, 1924):6.

43. Campbell, *Popular Lectures and Addresses,* p. 268. For an outline of the sources of his thought, see West, *Alexander Campbell and Natural Religion,* pp. 220-221.

44. Campbell, *Popular Lectures and Addresses,* pp. 90, 140, 225, 244, 303-307, 353; See also Campbell's "Baccalaureate Address. Delivered July 4th, to the Graduating Class of Bethany College," *Millennial Harbinger* (1849): 433, quoted by Perry Epler Gresham, *Campbell and the Colleges,* The Forrest F. Reed Lectures for 1971 (Nashville, Tennessee: The Disciples of Christ Historical Society, 1973):46.

45. For gods, Campbell, *Popular Lectures and Addresses,* pp. 307-308. See also *Millennial Harbinger* (1839):448; for Bible philosophers, pp. 303, 309; for the universe, pp. 97, 162, 187.

46. Gresham, *op. cit.;* note references on p. viii regarding doctoral dissertations.

47. Zollars, *The Commission Executed,* p. 11. The story about Dr. Johnson was told to me by Malcolm L. Norment in 1937.

48. Campbell, *Popular Lectures and Addresses,* pp. 240-241, 403; *Cf.* pp. 91-94, Zollars, *The Commission Executed,* p. 209; Edward Scribner Ames, *Religion* (New York: Red Label Reprints, c. 1929):245; See also pp. 243-249.

49. The phrase "aristocracy of merit" appeared in the prospectus for Oklahoma Christian University, opened in 1907, and in the catalogs of the school (now Phillips University) for decades; See Ronald E. Osborn, *Ely Vaughn Zollars, Teacher of Preachers, Builder of Colleges: A Biography* (St. Louis: Christian Board of Publication, 1947), p. 24. Campbell, *Popular Lectures and Addresses,* p. 507; See pp. 247, 250-51, 254. For an idealistic expression at the turn of the century, see "Our Liberty in Christ," a sermon preached at the inauguration of Burris A. Jenkins as president of Kentucky (Now Transylvania) University, in Powell, *The Victory of Faith,* pp. 114-128. For an essay in pragmatism see Ralph Waldo Nelson, *Free Minds: A Venture in the Philosophy of Democracy* (Washington, D. C.: Public Affairs Press, 1961).

50. William Warren Sweet, *Religion in the Development of American Culture, 1765-1840* (New York: Charles Scribner's Sons, 1952):165-166.

51. Campbell, *Popular Lectures and Addresses,* p. 251. Garfield, acceptance of Republican nomination, in Hinsdale, *The Republican Text-Book for the Campaign of 1880,* p. 150. Lindsay, "The Illinois Village," *op. cit.,* p. 74; *cf.* Jones, *A Man Stood up to Preach,* p. 219.

52. J. H. Garrison, address inaugurating the Bible College of Missouri, Jan. 21, 1896. See also Ronald B. Flowers, "The Bible Chair Movement: An Innovation of the Disciples of Christ," *Discipliana* (March, 1966):8-13, and "The Disciples of Christ Bible Chair at the University of Michigan," *ibid.*, (Summer, 1977):21-26, 30.

53. For elaboration of the issues, see my paper, "E. V. Zollars, the College, and the Church," *Bulletin of Hiram College* 59 (Nov., 1957).

54. B. A. Hinsdale, *President Garfield and Education: Hiram College Memorial* (Boston: James R. Osgood and Company, 1882):43, 365-426. For tribute to A. S. Fisher of Eureka College, see Nathaniel S. Haynes, *History of the Disciples of Christ in Illinois, 1819-1914* (Cincinnati: The Standard Publishing Company, 1915):37.

55. From notes made by the author on the back of the chapel program, March 2, 1939.

56. Hinsdale, *op. cit.*, p. 122.

57. B. A. Hinsdale, *Jesus as a Teacher, and The Making of the New Testament* (St. Louis: Christian Publishing Company, 1895):1.

58. Campbell, *The Christian System*, pp. 82-84.

59. Hinsdale, *Jesus as a Teacher*, p. 233; Alexander Procter, *The Witness of Jesus and Other Sermons;* with a biographical sketch by T. P. Haley; ed. J. H. Garrison (St. Louis: Christian Publishing Company, 1901):38-39.

60. Campbell, *Popular Lectures and Addresses*, p. 89; Elizabeth Ross, *Altar Songs* (Cincinnati, Ohio: Powell & White, 1925):22. Lindsay, *op. cit.*, p. 73.

61. Edgar DeWitt Jones, *Fairhope: The Annals of a Country Church*, frontispiece by Herbert Deland Williams (New York: The Macmillan Company, 1919), "A Hound of the Lord," pp. 89-99; Procter, *op. cit.*, pp. 14, 30, 85-87, 377-378.

62. Edward Scribner Ames, "Theory in Practice," reprinted from *Contemporary American Theology*, ed. Vergilius Ferm, Vol. II (New York: Round Table Press, Inc., 1933):10. See also Ames, *Beyond Theology*, pp. 30, 46-47, 56-60, 66, 68, 75, 80-83, 148, 198-199, 202, 211, 221.

63. Edgar DeWitt Jones, "Pulpit Princes of the Disciples of Christ," *Shane Quarterly* 12 (Oct., 1951):172-179. Fred B. Craddock has formulated a theology of preaching which takes seriously the freedom of the hearers and which undertakes through the very form and movement of the sermon to involve them in reaching conclusions for themselves instead of being handed authoritative conclusions from the pulpit; see his book, *As One Without Authority: Essays on Inductive Preaching*, rev. ed. (Enid, Oklahoma: The Phillips University Press, 1974).

64. Sweet, *op. cit.*, p. 186. J. H. Garrison, "What We Stand For" *The Christian-Evangelist* 38 (April 4, 1901):418.

65. A. McLean, *A Circuit of the Globe: A Series of Letters of Travel across the American Continent, through the Hawaiian Republic, Japan, China, The Straits Settlements, Burma, India, Ceylon, Australia, Egypt, Palestine, Syria, Turkey, Greece, Italy, Switzerland, Germany, Scandinavia, France, and England;* intro. by J. H. Garrison (St. Louis: Christian Publishing Company, 1897); Stephen J. England, *Oklahoma Christians: A History of Christian Churches and of the Start of the Christian Church (Disciples of Christ) in Oklahoma* ([St. Louis:] The Bethany Press, 1975):154-157.

66. Dwight E. Stevenson, *Lexington Theological Seminary, 1865-1965, The College of the Bible Century* (St. Louis, Missouri: The Bethany Press, 1964): 165-207. For developments elsewhere see Ronald E. Osborn, "Portrait of a Churchman: The Ministry of O. L. Shelton," *Encounter* 20 (Spring, 1959): 145-149; *Cf.* Zollars, *The Commission Executed*, p. 109.

67. Ames, *Beyond Theology*, pp. 193-202.

68. Blakemore, *The Renewal of Church: The Panel Reports*, I, 8, 11-12.

69. See Walter W. Sikes, *The Stranger in My House* (St. Louis, Missouri: The Bethany Press, 1957); *On Becoming the Truth: An Introduction to the Life and Thought of Sören Kierkegaard* (St. Louis, Missouri: The Bethany Press, 1968); "Explorations in Theology: Eight Articles by Walter W. Sikes," *Encounter* 33 (Winter, 1972). For one aspect of his leadership, see Samuel C. Pearson, Jr., "The Association of Disciples for Theological Discussion: A Brief Historical Appraisal," *Encounter* 37 (Summer, 1976):263ff.

70. Paul A. Crow, Jr., "George G. Beazley, Jr.: One of a Kind Ecumenist," *Mid-Stream* 16 (April, 1977):149-156. George G. Beazley, Jr. "A Visit with the Russian Orthodox Church," *News on Christian Unity* 13 (Nov. 19, 1973):5; Beazley, (ed.), *The Christian Church (Disciples of Christ): An Interpretative Examination in the Cultural Context* (St. Louis: The Bethany Press, 1973). Consult *Mid-Stream, passim.*

71. "William Barnett Blakemore, Jr., 1912-1975," *Bulletin of the Disciples Divinity House of the University of Chicago* 47 (Summer, 1975): 1, 3. Dean Blakemore's books include *The Cornerstone and the Builders: Essays on the Minister as Churchman,* Christian Foundation Lectures delivered in Emmanuel College, The University of Toronto, 1955 (Toronto: College of Churches of Christ in Canada); *Encountering God* (St. Louis: The Bethany Press, 1965); *The Discovery of the Church: A History of Disciple Ecclesiology,* The Reed Lectures for 1965 (Nashville, Tennessee: Reed and Company, 1966); *Quest for Intelligence in Ministry: The Story of the First Seventy-Five Years of the Disciples Divinity House of the University of Chicago* (Chicago: The Disciples Divinity House of the University of Chicago, 1970). He edited *The Challenge of Christian Unity,* The William Henry Hoover Lectures for 1961 (St. Louis, Missouri: The Bethany Press, 1963) and *The Renewal of Church: The Panel Reports.*

Lecture 3, Freedom for a United Church: The Integrity of the People of God

1. Garrison, *The Quest and Character of a United Church.* In his Garrison Lectures at Yale Divinity School in 1960, Walter W. Sikes dealt discerningly with many of the issues which I am addressing in Lecture 3; see his "The Principle of Authority and the Heritage of a Free Church," *Encounter* 33 (Winter, 1972):112-127.

2. Campbell, *Popular Lectures and Addresses,* p. 502. Flora Lewis, "Spain Communist leader compares new ideology to Christian church," (New York Times News Service), *The Oregonian,* July 8, 1976.

3. *Last Will and Testament of the Springfield Presbytery. Cf.* William Garrett West, *Barton Warren Stone, Early American Advocate of Christian Unity* (Nashville, Tennessee: The Disciples of Christ Historical Society, 1954): 17, 70.

4. William Herbert Hanna, *Thomas Campbell, Seceder and Christian Union Advocate* (Cincinnati: The Standard Publishing Company, 1935): 31-67. *Cf.* Lester G. McAllister, *Thomas Campbell, Man of the Book* (St. Louis, Missouri: The Bethany Press, 1954):72-95.

5. See Robert Richardson, *Memoirs of Alexander Campbell, Embracing a View of the Origin, Progress and Principles of the Religious Reformation Which He Advocated* (Philadelphia: J. B. Lippincott & Co., 1870), Vol. II, p. 137.

6. Wrather, *History in Stone and Stained Glass for The Thomas W. Phillips Memorial,* p. 9.

7. F. W. Burnham, "The Future of Free Churches," *The Christian-Evangelist*

77 (Sept. 21, 1939):1012-1014; *Cf.* The Disciple contributions to Harlan Paul Douglass (ed.), *The Witness of the Churches of the Congregational Order,* Papers Exchanged by Baptists, Congregational-Christians and Disciples in 1940 (Indianapolis: The Association for the Promotion of Christian Unity, 1940). See also Murch, *The Free Church.* For the Baptist manifesto, see "Charter of Freedom," *The Christian-Evangelist* (January 7, 1948):8; Howard Elmo Short, "The Contributions of Separatism to American Life," in Edwin T. Dahlberg (ed.), *Herald of the Evangel* (St. Louis, Missouri: The Bethany Press, 1965), pp. 143-144.

8. Winfred Ernest Garrison, "Creeds and Unity," *The Christian-Evangelist* 88 (July 19, 1950):698-700. See also his *caveat* about emerging directions in restructure, *A Fork in the Road: A Penetrating Analysis of Decisions Facing Disciples* (Indianapolis: Pension Fund of Christian Churches, 1964). A. T. DeGroot, *Extra ecclesiam nulla salus* (or, *Restructure Problems*), 2nd printing (Fort Worth, Texas: Author, 1969). Professor DeGroot had earlier (1966) issued the essay which appears as chapter II of this book in separate form, complete with cartoon. It was entitled "Episcopacy, in Succession."

9. W. E. Garrison, "Why I Continue to be a Disciple," *The First Christian,* Portland, Oregon (date detached. The article is obviously a reprint, but the source is not indicated).

10. "Original faith and order," A. Campbell, *The Christian System,* p. 10. *Cf. Popular Lectures and Addresses,* pp. 395, 537, 542-544, 560. "Rubbish of ages," Thomas Campbell, in *Declaration and Address and The Last Will and Testament of the Springfield Presbytery,* p. 19. For open membership in the tradition of Stone, see Tucker and McAllister, *Journey in Faith,* p. 377.

11. For Campbell's parable of the iron bedstead, see the *Christian Baptist* 4 (August 7, 1826):277ff. For the controversy over open communion, see Tucker and McAllister, *op. cit.,* p. 240-242. For the "catholic" argument, see my paper, " 'One Holy Catholic and Apostolic Church': The Continuing Witness of Disciples of Christ," in Blakemore, *The Renewal of Church: The Panel Reports,* I, 336-339. For a statement by the Disciples' modern pioneer of ecumenism, see Peter Ainslie, *The Message of the Disciples for the Union of the Church, Including Their Origin and History,* Lectures delivered before the Yale Divinity School, New Haven (New York: Fleming H. Revell Company, 1913), chap. 1.

12. W. J. Lhamon, *An Address to the Members of the Commission for the Restudy of the Disciples of Christ, and more broadly to our Disciple Fellowship at large* (pamphlet. Columbia, Missouri: Author, n.d. [ca. 1943]). Ralph G. Wilburn, "A Critique of the Restoration Principle: Its Place in Contemporary Life and Thought," in Blakemore, *The Renewal of Church: The Panel Reports,* I, 215-253; *Cf.* my paper, "For Freedom Christ Has Set Us Free: The Insufficiency of the Restoration Principle and the Sufficiency of Christ the Lord," in Charles R. Gresham (ed.), *Consultation on Internal Unity of Christian Churches,* Meeting at St. Louis, Missouri, February 27-29, 1964 (Fifth Series):58-72. For a conservative statement in which restoration has become the unarticulated, though not disavowed, member of the triad, see James E. Smith, "Freedom Is Unity," *Christian Standard* 111 (1976):820-822, 844-846, 868-870.

13. West, *Alexander Campbell and Natural Religion,* chap. II, "The Clergy and Their Kingdom." For Peter Cartwright, see H. Richard Niebuhr and Daniel D. Williams (eds.), *The Ministry in Historical Perspectives* (New York: Harper & Brothers Publishers, 1956):239. For Cumberland Presbyterians, see Sweet, *Religion in the Development of American Culture,* pp. 216-219.

14. Campbell, *The Christian System,* pp. 82-90; William Martin Smith, *Servants without Hire: Emerging Concepts of the Christian Ministry in the Campbell-Stone Movement,* The Reed Lectures for 1967 (Nashville, Tennessee: The Disciples of Christ Historical Society, 1968); See also my paper, "The Eldership among Disciples of Christ," *Mid-Stream* 6 (Winter, 1967), 74-112. For theological reflection on ministry see my book, *In Christ's Place: Christian Ministry in Today's World* (St. Louis, Missouri: The Bethany Press, 1967), Chap. 9, "Ordination: Appointment to Public Ministry."

15. Consider, for example, the recently organized Congress of Disciples Clergy and its journal *Foci* (available from Christian Church Services, Inc., P. O. Box 1986, Indianapolis, Indiana 46206).

16. "The Christian Church inducts into the order of its ministry men and women . . . , "A Provisional Design for the Christian Church (Disciples of Christ)," para. 95. For Campbell's use of Scripture to oppose women as ministers, see Shaw, *Buckeye Disciples,* p. 112. For the case favoring ordination of women, see Mossie Allman Wyker, *Church Women in the Scheme of Things,* (St. Louis, Missouri: The Bethany Press, 1953), chap. 3, "The Church Woman and Ordination." See *Women in the Church: A Symposium on the Service and Status of Women among the Disciples of Christ* (Lexington, Kentucky: The College of the Bible, 1953). In 1962, 20 women served as pastors; in 1972, 14; in 1977, 20, plus 13 as co-pastors. In 1962, 4 women served as associate pastors; in 1972, 6; in 1977, 44. This apparent increase is doubtless offset by the decline in the number of directors of Christian education, 126 women in 1962, 77 in 1972. The dramatic increase is in the number of women enrolled in theological seminaries, 140 Disciples in 1977. See "Women in the Ministry," Department of Ministry and Worship, Division of Homeland Ministries, 1972; "An Update of Statistics for Women's Participation in the Christian Church (Disciples of Christ)," Department of Church Women, 1974. For the 1977 statistics I am indebted to Nancy T. Helmer of the Division of Homeland Ministries, letter of August 9, 1977.

17. See my paper, "Ordained Ministry for a Vital Church—Some Theological and Practical Reflections," *Mid-Stream* 13 (Spring-Sum., 1974):71-95.

18. For the views of Madison and Jefferson on opinion, see Sidney E. Mead, *The Nation with the Soul of a Church* (New York: Harper & Row, Publishers, 1975):119-122. The convergence of rationalism and pietism is discussed in Carey J. Gifford's paper, "Whig and Jacksonian Politics, and Alexander Campbell," p. 22; *Cf.* Niebuhr and Williams, *The Ministry in Historical Perspectives,* p. 211.

19. Campbell, *Popular Lectures and Addresses,* p. 304, 591; For Scott, see Stevenson, *Walter Scott, Voice of the Golden Oracle: A Biography,* pp. 32-36. *Cf.* Dwight E. Stevenson, "Faith Versus Theology in the Thought of the Disciple Fathers," in Blakemore *The Renewal of Church: The Panel Reports,* I, 33-60; *Cf.* "Where We Stand," by Robert Richardson, condensed and introduced by Dwight E. Stevenson, *The Christian-Evangelist* 85 (1947):111-112, 138-139, 183-184. On the early downgrading of theology, see West, *Alexander Campbell and Natural Religion,* pp. 16, 29-44, 117, 130-132, 219-221.

20. Zollars, *The Commission Executed,* p. viii; Hinsdale, *Garfield-Hinsdale Letters,* pp. 134-135.

21. For the liberal reformulation, see my chapter, "Theology among the Disciples," in Beazley, *The Christian Church (Disciples of Christ): An Interpretative History,* especially pp. 101-108. For a twentieth century statement of the anti-creedal position, see A. Campbell Garnett, *A Realistic Philosophy of Religion* (Chicago: Willett, Clark & Company, 1942):147-150, 181-184, 194.

22. Early in the twentieth century many congregations used a hymnal which contained among its aids to worship "A Scriptural Confession of Faith" and even the Apostle's Creed; see Charles Clayton Morrison and Herbert L. Willett (eds.), *Hymns of the United Church* (Chicago: The Christian Century Press, c. 1919, p. 425. (For allusion to this as "the new Disciples' hymnal," see Machlachlan's paper in Willett, Jordan, and Sharpe, *Progress,* p. 179). Dean Blakemore's Task Committee presented to the Commission on Restructure "A Booklet Looking Toward the Preparation for Brotherhood-Wide Use of Declarations or Acknowledgments or Affirmations of The Covenant Which God Has Made with His People and by Which We Are Bound Together as His Church of Christ on Earth," (June 21, 1965). For recent expressions on creeds, see *Jesus Christ Frees and Unites: A Summary of Responses of Congregations of the Christian Church (Disciples of Christ) to the Theme of the Fifth Assembly of the World Council of Churches* (Indianapolis, Indiana: Council on Christian Unity, 1975):1-2, 6; See also my paper, "Confession and Catholicity: The Rightful Function of Creeds in the Life of the Church," *Mid-Stream* 16 (April, 1977):198-205. For creeds in the projections of the Consultation on Church Union, see *A Plan of Union* (1970), chap. V, para. 9-11.

23. Frederick A. Henry, *Captain Henry of Geauga: A Family Chronicle* (Cleveland: The Gates Press, 1942):348.

24. For a review of Disciple ecclesiology, see D. Ray Lindley, "The Structure of the Church: Freedom and Authority in Matters of Polity" in Blakemore (ed.), *The Renewal of Church: The Panel Reports,* I, 184-198. For older treatises on polity, see Thomas Munnell, *The Care of All the Churches* (St. Louis: Christian Publishing Co., 1888); W. L. Hayden, *Church Polity: A Practical Treatise on The Organization and Regulation of the Kingdom of God on Earth, as Set Forth in the New Testament* (Chicago: S. J. Clarke, 1894).

25. Zollars, *The Commission Executed,* p. 224.

26. Wayne H. Bell, "A History of Vine Street Christian Church," in *Seven Early Churches of Nashville,* a series of lectures presented at The Public Library of Nashville and Davidson County (Nashville, Tennessee: Elder's Bookstore, 1972):88-89. In a letter of July 12, 1976, Henry K. Shaw comments eloquently on the way in which the exercise of personal power sometimes overrode freedom in the congregations.

27. For unsuccessful attempts to deal with the problem, see Shaw, *Buckeye Disciples,* p. 124; Garrison and DeGroot, *The Disciples of Christ: A History,* p. 246. For current procedure, see *A Provisional Design,* para. 93-101; *Cf.* the document approved by the 1971 General Assembly, Resolution #49, "Concerning Policies and Criteria for the Order of Ministry in the Christian Church (Disciples of Christ," in George Earle Owen and Clora S. Keltner (eds.), *1972 Year Book and Directory of the Christian Church (Disciples of Christ): Reports for the Last Year (July 1, 1970-June 30, 1971)* (Indianapolis, Indiana: The General Office of the Christian Church [Disciples of Christ], 1972):186-190.

28. See "A Response to Lund: Response of Disciples of Christ in the United States and Canada to the Report of the Third World Conference on Faith and Order, Lund, Sweden, 1952," Drafted by the Faith and Order Committee of the Association for the Promotion of Christian Unity (Disciples of Christ), *Shane Quarterly* 14 (July, 1953):91ff. (issued also as undated reprint). For the difficulty of participating in ecumenical dialog without an ecclesiastical base, see Robert O. Fife, "Christian Unity as Reception and Attainment," in Robert O. Fife, David Edwin Harrell, Jr., and Ronald E. Osborn, *Disciples and the Church Universal,* The Forrest F. Reed Lectures for 1966 (Nashville, Tennessee: The Disciples of Christ Historical Society, 1967):10-11, 26-27.

29. A recent poll addressed to the minister and three lay office-holders in each congregation of one region drew 277 replies (a return rate of 61.5%). Of these, 81% reported that their congregations accept members on the basis of any previous baptism and church membership. "Report of the Southern California-Southern Nevada Regional Study Committee on Mutual Recognition of Members," April 1, 1977.

30. Eva Jean Wrather, *Creative Freedom in Action: Alexander Campbell on the Structure of the Church* (St. Louis, Missouri: The Bethany Press, 1968); *Cf.* Shaw, *Buckeye Disciples,* p. 114. Ronald E. Osborn, "The Structure of Cooperation: Its Development in the History and Thought of Disciples of Christ." *Mid-Stream* 2 (Dec., 1962): 28-49. Ronald E. Osborn, *Restructure . . . Toward the Christian Church (Disciples of Christ): Intention, Essence, Constitution, and a statement by the Commission on Brotherhood Restructure, Louisville, Kentucky, June 29 to July 1, 1964)* (St. Louis: Christian Board of Publication, 1964); Loren E. Lair, *The Christian Churches and Their Work* (St. Louis: The Bethany Press, 1963); Lair, *The Christian Church (Disciples of Christ) and Its Future* (St. Louis, Missouri: The Bethany Press, 1971).

31. "Strategy of World Missions," The United Christian Missionary Society (mimeographed), 1953. *Cf.* Virgil A. Sly, "Participation in United Churches," *World Call* (March, 1955): 10-13.

32. Murch, *Christians Only,* pp. 256-259.

33. W. B. Blakemore, "Autonomy? NO! Independency? YES!" *The Christian-Evangelist* (October 14, 1953): 982-986, and subsequent commentary, *passim.*

34. *A Provisional Design,* para. 3, 72, 87-90. "Response to 'A Plan of Union for the Church of Christ Uniting' From the Christian Church (Disciples of Christ)," *The Christian* (1972):1028-1033.

35. W. B. Blakemore, "Campbell Out-Campbellited," *The Scroll* 47 (1949): 131-132. Campbell, *Popular Lectures and Addresses,* p. 308; *Cf.* Hunter Beckelhymer, "Representative Preaching about Jesus: Two Generations of the Middle Period," in Blakemore, *Renewal of Church: The Panel Reports,* I, chap. 4. "Christ Centered Religion," Bulletin of First Christian Church, Orange, Calif., October 10, 1948, accompanied by letter (Oct. 11) from Willis M. Whitaker, minister. *Cf.* W. A. Visser't Hooft," The Christocentric Character of the Ecumenical Movement," *Mid-Stream* 16 (April, 1977): 157-169.

36. Lin D. Cartwright, *The Great Commitment: The Meaning of the Confession of Faith* (St. Louis, Missouri: The Bethany Press, 1962):117-120.

37. C. C. Morrison, "Why I Am a Disciple," *The Christian-Evangelist* 86 (June 30, 1948):649.

38. Campbell, *Popular Lectures and Addresses,* p. 537; *The Christian System,* p. 10. Archibald McLean, *Where the Book Speaks, Or Mission Studies in the Bible* (New York: Fleming H. Revell Company, 1907). For racism, see Kring Allen, "Integration by the Cross," *The Christian Century* (Aug. 20, 1958):943-945; *Cf.* the biblical witness within the Church of Christ against racism as reported in D.R. Cutler, *The Religious Situation 1969* (Boston: Beacon Press, 1969):1077. My colleague, Professor Loren Fisher has dealt refreshingly and pertinently with such current issues as ecology and sexism in his public lectures on the Old Testament, e.g., "Mankind in Creation," (April 16, 1974), exegeting principles of liberating power by examining the text in the context of the ancient worldview and other contemporaneous literatures.

39. John B. Cowden in *Saint Paul on Christian Unity* wrote in a traditional Disciple vein: "The Catholic Church has unity without liberty; and the

Protestant Church has liberty without unity; but the Apostolic Church had unity with liberty, which was realized and maintained through loyalty." (p. 188). W. E. Garrison in *The Quest and Character of a United Church,* elaborated this thesis with reference to the ecumenical movement. For Troeltsch, see James C. Livingston, *Modern Christian Thought, from the Enlightenment to Vatican II* (New York: The Macmillan Company, 1971): 305.

40. For Ainslie, see Homer W. Carpenter, review of *On This Rock* by G. Bromley Oxnam, *The Christian-Evangelist* 89 (May 9, 1951):455.

41. Hampton Adams, address on "Disciples and the Ecumenical Principle," School of Religion, Butler University, July 22, 1953, as recorded in author's notes. William Robinson, "The Church—A Disciple Point of View," *The Christian-Evangelist* 84 (Feb. 13, 1946):174. *Cf.* Cowden, *Saint Paul on Christian Unity,* p. 187: "Liberty, loyalty, and unity constitute the Scriptural Trinity of the New Testament Church."

42. For a general analysis and commentary, see The Worship Study Commission (1966-1969), Department of Ministry and Worship, *Worship in the Christian Church: The Common Worship of the Church* (Indianapolis: The United Christian Missionary Society for The Christian Church [Disciples of Christ], 1969). *Cf.* G. Edwin Osborn (ed.), *Christian Worship: A Service Book* (St. Louis: Christian Board of Publication, 1953); Keith Watkins, *The Breaking of Bread: An Approach to Worship for the Christian Churches (Disciples of Christ)* (St. Louis, Missouri: The Bethany Press, 1966). For theological reflection on the sacraments, see the report of the Commission on Theology and Christian Unity produced under a mandate from the International Convention of Christian Churches (Disciples of Christ): Baptism and the Lord's Supper: Materials for Restudy," *Mid-Stream* 5 (Winter, 1965).

43. For rapid growth of churches through conversion of adults, see Timothy L. Smith, *Revivalism and Social Reform in Mid-Nineteenth-Century America* (Nashville: Abingdon Press, 1957):59. For idyllic accounts of baptisms, see Jones, *Fairhope: The Annals of a Country Church,* pp. 50-55; Wasson, *James A. Garfield: His Religion and Education,* p. 50; Ware, *History of the Disciples of Christ in California,* pp. 63-65. For recent studies, see Stephen J. England, *The One Baptism: Baptism and Christian Unity with Special Reference to Disciples of Christ* (St. Louis, Mo.: The Bethany Press, 1960); also his paper, "Toward a Theology of Baptism," in Blakemore, *The Renewal of Church: The Panel Reports,* III, 189-226; J. Daniel Joyce, *The Place of the Sacraments in Worship* (St. Louis, Missouri: The Bethany Press, 1967), chap. 6.

44. See Keith Watkins, "An Order for the Celebration of the Great Thanksgiving" in John C. Kirby, *Word and Action: New Forms of the Liturgy* (New York: The Seabury Press, 1969), pp. 171-179; *Cf.* Professor Watkins' rationale for this order, and commentary by several liturgical authorities, in *Encounter* 24 (Summer, 1963). For recent theological studies, see Blakemore, "Worship and the Lord's Supper" in *the Renewal of Church: The Panel Reports,* III, 227-250; Joyce, *The Place of the Sacraments in Worship,* chap. 7.

45. COCU, *A Plan of Union,* chap. VII, para. 56. The continuing prominence of elders in the ministry of the Lord's table, long after the other ministerial duties they once exercised have been taken over by a professional pastor (an ordained member of the "clergy"), has led many Disciples to put a new interpretation on their role. Whereas Campbell insisted that the elders constituted one of the three orders of the standing and immutable ministry and that they should be ordained to their office, most Disciples now see

them as representative *lay* members, sharing with the pastor the presidency of the eucharistic celebration, or even exercising it in their own right. This perception has resulted in the widespread inference that presiding at the table is proper for any Christian who may be designated by the church for a particular occasion. (This is a quite different matter from a person's assuming the presidency on one's own initiative.) This right is repeatedly asserted as part of the Disciples' witness to the priesthood of believers and to freedom from clericalism, though the congregation would be rare where it is exercised more than two or three times a year. The view of Christian freedom held by most Disciples sees no problem in this practice, nor any obstacle to church union. See "Response to *A Plan of Union* . . . ," *The Christian,* 110 (Aug. 13, 1972):9:

Any baptized Christian who is worthy and who is designated by the congregation may preside over a given celebration of the Eucharist without ordination.

Cf. Mary Lou Canedy, *No Skeletons in Our Closet: CMF/CWF Group Studies for 1977-78* (St. Louis, Missouri: Christian Board of Publication, 1977):49:

Another beautiful teaching of the Christian Church is that communion is not the sole province of the ordained clergy but can be served by designated lay persons in any service. We are on the forefront in seeing communion as an ecumenical expression that frees and unites. Your local church has practiced this since its inception and will continue to do so.

Cf. "Response of the Christian Church (Disciples of Christ) to *One Baptism, One Eucharist and a Mutual[ly] Recognized Ministry* (World Council of Churches Commission on Faith and Order), approved by the Executive Committee of the Council on May 9, 1977 (Indianapolis: Council on Christian Unity, Xeroxed):2:

We would draw attention to the practice we have whereby any member of the congregation may take part in the prayers of the Church at the Lord's Table. We have found this helpful in affirming that the prayers offered are those of the whole body.

See also the section in "Ministry" in this response.

Prof. Keith Watkins has commented discerningly on the widespread understanding of the elders as *lay* persons sharing in a "bicameral ministry" at the table; "Ministry in the Christian Church" (July 1, 1977, unpublished paper).

46. O. L. Shelton, "The Nature of the Church," address at the Richmond Indiana State Convention of the churches, May 15-18, 1955 (pamphlet), *Cf.* Dean Shelton's series of articles elaborating this concept: "How Shall We Think of the Church?" *The Christian-Evangelist* (1957):42-43, 76-77, 107-108.
47. *A Provisional Design,* para. 3, 7, 92. *Cf.* The chapters on "Structure" and "Covenant" in Kenneth L. Teegarden, *We Call Ourselves Disciples* (St. Louis, Missouri: The Bethany Press, 1975):57-73; my study, *In Christ's Place,* chap. 8, "The Body and Its Ordering: The Anatomy of Servanthood."
48. *A Provisional Design,* para. 33.
49. *Cf.* my article, "Religious Freedom and the Form of the Church: An Assessment of the Denomination in America," *Lexington Theological Quarterly* 11 (July, 1976):85-106.
50. *A Provisional Design,* para. 88, 89.

Both the congregation and the denomination of course, wield some power with respect to ministers, but it is essentially economic and related to their advancement in their careers.

51. "Nothing can be moral that is not voluntary," Dean E. Walker in an unpublished letter, quoted by William Judson Richardson, "Toward Christian Unity," four lectures given at the Oregon Christian Missionary Convention in 1951 (mimeographed), p. 16; *Cf.* "Response to A Plan of Union," *The Christian* (Aug. 13, 1972):5-6, "A Tradition of Freedom."
52. Moore, *A Comprehensive History of the Disciples of Christ,* p. 808.
53. John 8:36 *(The Living Oracles).*

INDEX

140

141

Northwest Christian College, 15, 16